History and Identity

American Academy of Religion
Studies in Religion

edited by
Conrad Cherry

Number 19
History and Identity
by Sidney E. Mead

History and Identity

Sidney E. Mead

Scholars Press

Distributed by
Scholars Press
PO Box 5207
Missoula, Montana 59806

History and Identity

by

Sidney E. Mead

Library of Congress Cataloging in Publication Data

Mead, Sidney Earl, 1904–
  History and identity.

  (American Academy of Religion studies in religion ;
19 ISSN 0084-6287)
  Includes bibliographical references.
  1. Identification (Religion) 2. History (Theology)
3. Church history—Philosophy. I. Title. II. Series:
American Academy of Religion. AAR studies in
religion ; 19.
BV4509.5.M38   230   78-26543
ISBN 0-89130-274-3
ISBN 0-89130-297-2 pbk.

Printed in the United States of America

1   2   3   4   5   6

Edwards Brothers, Inc.
Ann Arbor, MI 48104

DEDICATION

I would say with Montaigne that ". . . if these essays were worthy of being judged, I think they might not be much liked by common and vulgar minds, or by singular and excellent ones; the former would not understand enough about them, the latter too much. But they might get by in the middle region."
So I dedicate them

TO ALL THOSE WHO DWELL WITH ME
"IN THE MIDDLE REGION"

CONTENTS

INTRODUCTION

Sidney E. Mead is an accomplished master of the essay in historical interpretation. He brings together the industry and rigor of honest research, the creativity of a disciplined imagination, and the strength of a polished literary style. "My ideal historian is a creative artist,"[1] he writes; as a crown of a lifetime of labor he approaches his own ideal. Many of his essays were often given first as addresses or lectures, became articles in periodicals or chapters in books, and then were collected in a series of volumes: *The Lively Experiment: The Shaping of Christianity in America* (1963), *The Nation with the Soul of a Church* (1975), *The Old Religion in the Brave New World: Reflections on the Relation Between Christendom and the Republic* (1977), and *Love and Learning* (1978).[2] Many scholars have paid tribute to the influence he has had upon them; for example, Edwin S. Gaustad has recently written,

> And to another good teacher, Sidney E. Mead, I owe much. While I was never "his" student in any formal sense, I have gained more from chance encounters, hallway conversations, and helpful letters than one has any right to expect.[3]

I *was* his student in a formal sense, and have continued through the decades to learn much from his writings and from the exchanges, some by chance and some by design, in correspondence, hallway conversations, and meetings of historical societies.

Throughout his long career as historian of religion in America, Mead has wrestled with the issues of the philosophy and theology of history. I well remember my first encounter with him in 1944; his course on "Christian Thought in America" began with a thorough examination of the purposes for studying religious history and of the premises, conscious and unconscious, which the historian brings to the work of narration and interpretation. His interest in these and related matters has continued through the years; his wide and interdisciplinary reading has enriched his search for a fuller understanding of self and others, of historical events and ultimate truth. The present book brings together four of his mature contributions to a significant discussion among historians, philosophers, and theologians—one that we hope continues and that will be further stimulated by this collection.

Mead is aware that his is a personal quest for identity and meaning; he has not hesitated to use the first person singular throughout these reflections. Yet he is searching for truth in the largest sense, and has a skillful way of pressing his readers to see what he has seen, and to take it as seriously as he has. Those of us who may disagree in matters small or large with what he

1

presents can hardly fail to be informed and challenged by his intellectual power and interpretative artistry.

The essays that make up this volume were published over a span of more than a decade. Each writing has its own distinctive theme and development, yet certain common motifs are elaborated throughout, for example:

The student of history is seeking self-knowledge and self-understanding, which will bring a larger measure of genuine freedom, and rescue one from the dangers and immobilities of the "terrible freedom" of modern life with its pluralistic complexities.

Historical existence forces on one the necessity of choosing, implicitly or explicitly, a religion, a faith.

Interpretations of reality that emphasize its unity and continuity are more adequate than those that are dualistic, that separate "inner" from "outer" history, or that divide intellectual from religious quests.

The idea of incarnation is an important clue to understanding unity and continuity in the universe and in human life.

The individual finds a sense of identity, stability, and security in relation to some community—a church, a nation, humanity itself.

Though such common motifs are elaborated in these essays, still certain changes in the mind of such a searching and probing thinker as Mead are to be expected. The measure of change can be seen especially in the way the last two points are expounded from "On the Meaning of History" (1961) and "Church History Explained" (1963) to "History and Identity" (1971) and "American History as a Tragic Drama" (1972). The interpretation of incarnation moves from specific christological references to the general concept of the actualization of the creative idea in history. The search for community within which one finds the needed sense of identity and security shifts from a church ("too small, too circumscribed in time and space, too droopy in its thinking, too competitive, too involved in its own survival") or a nation ("the actuality of America appeared more and more ugly and less and less the progressive incarnation of the ideal") to an inclusive community unbroken for billions of years and including not only all "living" things but all "inorganic" matter as well.[4] Mead has found such a community in the writings of Loren Eiseley and others. How the individual responds to this pilgrimage from particular to general will depend on one's own philosophy of life, on one's faith. For me, who heard "History and Identity" when it was originally delivered, and was set off on a profitable season of reading Eiseley, this concept of community is so vast and inclusive as to become abstract. But whether one follows Mead in his journey closely or from a distance, one will find the mind stretched and imagination kindled in reading these illuminating and provocative essays. Not only historians, but those of many disciplines and interests who are concerned about the human past and future can find much here to inform and to excite them.

Robert T. Handy

NOTES

[1]See below, p. 39.

[2]A full bibliography is in *Love and Learning* (Chico, CA: New Horizons Press, 1978), pp. 111–22.

[3]In the Preface to his edition of Obadiah Holmes, *Baptist Piety: The Last Will and Testimony of Obadiah Holmes* (Grand Rapids, MI: Wm. B. Eerdmans Publ. Co., 1978), p. ix.

[4]See below, pp. 14, 51, 16.

PREFACE

These four essays bring together my reflections on the nature, the purpose, and the doing of history. If, with R. G. Collingwood, we define philosophy as reflective thinking, or thinking about the way we think,[1] or with J. Bronowski that it is taking a "critical attitude toward our own habits of thought,"[2] then I suppose they partake of philosophy. This led one of my keenest critics to describe me as "a philosopher and theologian who makes use of historical data."[3]

In a sense this is true. For inasmuch as method implies a metaphysics, every written history is implicitly a defense of the author's method. And because one must be somebody before he can be a historian, insofar as he reflects on who he is he is first philosopher and second historian. I have thought it a seemly thing for the historian to try to make his implicit philosophy or theology of history explicit. But I do not think that this makes him a philosopher or theologian in the technical sense of the words when they are used in referring to the university's artificial division of knowledge into disciplines. So I agree more with a second acute critic who said of me, "He is first and last a historian, not a theologizer about American history. . . ."[4]

Actually I have little concern about which academic pigeonhole readers stuff me into. But I note with a flicker of amusement that perhaps ever since the Lord God paraded the beasts and the birds before Adam "to see what he would call them," categorizing fellow workers in the academic vineyard has often passed for significant comment, especially among those existentially inclined sons of Adam who have noted that "whatsoever Adam called every living creature, that *was* the name thereof."

The four lectures here brought together are essays in both senses in which that word is used. On the one hand, each is an attempt to try out an idea and interpretation. On the other hand, each deals with a single subject from my personal point of view, without attempting to be exhaustive or definitive. Each is an interim report on how a topic looked to me at the particular time and place it was composed. In putting them together for this symposium we followed the nicely ambiguous suggestion of James Bryce that "An author who finds himself obliged to choose between repetition and obscurity ought not to doubt as to his choice."[5]

I have thought of myself primarily as a teacher with a passion to communicate ideas. In playing this role I have agreed with Whitehead that in abstraction ideas are "static, frozen, and lifeless. They obtain 'life and motion' by their entertainment in a living intelligence,"[6] as Homer's ghosts regained the power of speech only when given the fresh blood of recently slaughtered sheep.[7] The teacher is the living intelligence that brings life to ideas that for the students have being only in the limbo of the past. Unless the ideas are infused with the teacher's lifeblood they remain for the students static, lifeless, and useless in the form of temporarily memorized facts—something so common in academe as to lead Henry Adams to conclude that "Nothing in education is so astonishing as the amount of ignorance it accumulates in the form of inert facts."[8]

The central theme that runs through the four essays and gives unity to the collection is the relation of historical studies to the achievement of stable identity. Here I have built upon Erik H. Erikson's contention that one essential element in such achievement is the sense of solidarity with an historical people, a community that transcends the individual in both time and space and therefore meaningfully connects his past, present, and future. But I must let the essays speak for themselves.

Because of the diversity of backgrounds that called these essays into being it is impossible to acknowledge my indebtedness to the many individuals who contributed to them. But mention of the occasion for which each was prepared will carry, however obliquely, a note of gratitude for those who impelled me into making my reflections public. For never having been under the felt need to publish or perish, I think I have seldom produced anything unless prodded to do so by the necessities of classroom preparation or by an invitation to speak to a group.

"Church History Explained" was mothered by classroom attempts to orient students to my way of doing the history of America's religions and churches. "History and Identity" was finally licked into shape for a plenary session of the American Society of Church History. "American History as a Tragic Drama" was tried out in various forms and situations before it finally saw print because of the urging of friends and erstwhile colleagues at the Divinity School of the University of Chicago. "On the Meaning of History" was dashed off at the request of Martin E. Marty while he was wearing the purple fringed toga of an editor of *The Christian Century*, and obviously when I was on the one hand irritated by the, to me, monstrously incoherent historiography of an existentialist theologian, and, on the other hand, thrilled by the exuberant bulk and dash of G. K. Chesterton's writings.

Beyond this diffused acknowledgement of indebtedness and expression of gratitude, three persons must have special mention.

Professor Robert T. Handy, whose willingness to write an introduction gave the final push to publication, has for me during the past three decades played the roles of student, colleague, close and dependable friend—and during the many years of his distinguished career at Union Theological Seminary in New York has demonstrated to my parochial Midwestern soul that something good can come from east of the Hudson.

Mary Lou Doyle, as editor and friend, deserves unimaginable credit for tending to all the many technical details encountered along the rough road from writing to print—and withal, for the patience to do it for one she once, with customary keen discernment and to my great delight, called an irascible old man.

The fact that the publication date of this book will nearly coincide with the anniversary of our elopement fifty years ago makes it a tribute to Mildred LaDue Mead, for whom my appreciation must be expressed in other than words.

Sidney E. Mead
Tucson, Arizona
November 9, 1978

NOTES

[1] *The Idea of History* (Oxford: Clarendon Press, 1946), p. 1.
[2] *The Common Sense of Science* (New York: Vintage Books, n.d.), p. 102.
[3] Martin E. Marty, "The Two Religions of America," *Worldview*, 19, 3 (March 1976), 48.
[4] William A. Clebsch, "A New Historiography of American Religion," *Historical Magazine of the Protestant Episcopal Church*, XXXII, 3 (September 1963), 249.
[5] *The American Commonwealth* (3rd ed.; New York: Macmillan, 1908), p. 7.
[6] Alfred North Whitehead, *Adventures of Ideas* (New York: Free Press, 1967), p. 147.
[7] *The Odyssey*, Book XI.
[8] *The Education of Henry Adams* (Boston: Houghton Mifflin, 1918), p. 379.

I HISTORY AND IDENTITY[1]

The story of Eden is a greater allegory than man has ever guessed. For it was truly man who, walking memoryless through bars of sunlight and shade in the morning of the world, sat down and passed a wondering hand across his heavy forehead. Time and darkness, knowledge of good and evil, have walked with him ever since. . . .

For the first time in four billion years a living creature had contemplated himself and heard with a sudden, unaccountable loneliness, the whisper of the wind in the night reeds. Perhaps he knew, there in the grass by the chill waters, that he had before him an immense journey.[2]

Long ago and far away when I was still experiencing the metamorphosis from graduate student to faculty member and, being a child of depression, wondering at the munificent salary The University of Chicago was paying me for doing what I liked to do, I began to wonder why society paid me at all. You will recognize that this was the question of the purpose of teaching American religious history, formulated in the context of a functionalist approach. It meant, "What does the teaching of such history have to contribute to the functioning of our society?"

That question has haunted me ever since—my every course, my every class session. It has plagued the reading of examinations, papers, and dissertations. In the midst of the most routine duties of a professor I have asked myself with varying emphasis, "What am I doing here?"

For about five and twenty of my almost thirty years of teaching, during which I was responsible only for graduate students in theological schools and history departments, the answer was not too difficult. It could be assumed that the theologues were (or ought to be) headed toward the ministry, or if they had no stomach or talent for that, toward teaching in theological schools. The other students were headed toward doing research in, and teaching, history.

Then in 1964 I came to Iowa and for the first time encountered undergraduates. They came in large numbers, from every area of the university and from every social, economic, and religious background that our pluralistic society affords. Their infinite variety makes all generalizations about them suspect—a fact that vitiates many of the articles written about them. But there they were to be taught what I had to offer. I soon discovered that teaching undergraduates must proceed on premises different from those that have been almost adequate for graduate students.

For example, one thing the historian-teacher of graduate students has a right to assume is that his students have an interest in history and some

9

understanding of the purpose and methods of the discipline. Confronted with undergraduates, he cannot assume—and in our society has no sound reason for assuming—either such interest or such understanding. I was amused by the reported results of a study made at a major university some time ago. Financed, I suppose, by some foundation, the study was to find out whether an ideal introduction to American history could be developed. After considerable experimentation under controlled conditions, the directors solemnly concluded: (1) that one could not assume in American undergraduates a "natural" curiosity about the past; (2) that therefore the course had better be devoted to the cultivation of such curiosity—which meant that the course had better be not an introduction to American history but an introduction to historical thinking; (3) that under controlled conditions such a course probably could be developed; but (4) that it would be impossible for either faculty or students to do it in the context of a regular academic semester! I take it that the results suggest a good reason for not trying to change either the present content or methods of our traditional courses.

I agree with the first two conclusions "for substance thereof"—which means according to my understanding and interpretation of them.

The first, that one cannot assume a "natural" curiosity about the past on the part of his students, should have been obvious before an expensive experiment was launched to demonstrate it. In fact, granted aspects of our educational system, the wonder is that some students seem to survive secondary school with a modicum of intellectual curiosity intact.[3] Be that as it may, the attitude of many students toward the study of history is expressed in the inelegant question, "Why the hell should I?"

I think that question deserves a serious answer. It points, indeed, to the basic problem that lurks behind all teaching—the problem of how to motivate one's students to learn what one has to offer.

By and large in our society, and for a long time, the primary resort has been to overt or covert coercion. When my attention wandered in elementary school, the teacher spanked the palm of my hand with a brass-edged ruler—that was overt coercion. In graduate school the grading and financial awards systems had been substituted for the ruler—that is covert coercion. Neither seems to be an ideal way to instill either a love of learning or a self-propelled drive to learn.

The most effective substitute for coercion in teaching is the communication of the sense that what one has to offer is relevant to the student's living of *his* life. This, indeed, seems to me to be a primary purpose in teaching. We are all egoists, and when we are asked to do anything—including to learn something—it is natural that our first question is likely to be, "What is there in it *for me?*" The teacher should answer that question. And he should not assume, as many professors apparently do, that his students have, or ought to have, the same perspective and set of interests that he does.

The most simple form of the answer is, "Self-understanding—that is what there is in it for you." Or, as one student wrote me, "You reaffirmed my feeling that no amount of knowledge is worth two cents unless it somehow increases self-knowledge."

Whatever else it may be, a sense of identity is a matter of self-knowledge—or of understanding one's self.

The basic connotation of "identity," when applied to a person or group, is that of sameness, or oneness, that persists in time. When we speak of the identity of *a* person we point to those traits which he exhibits regularly over a period of time. There is no such thing as an instantaneous observation of character. A person is known only by his habitual acts, physical, mental, spiritual. Cognitively these outward, observable, persistent traits constitute the substance of his identity.[4]

From observation of such traits we form an opinion of his character, or unique identity. One does not directly observe the character either of another person or of one's self. The identity of an individual, including myself, is an intellectual construct in my mind—the result of reflection on observed traits that appear repeatedly in time. *My* sense of identity is the result of a conscious intellectual effort to interpret the meaning of my habitual modes of thinking and acting. I am assuming, of course, that there is no sense of identity apart from self-consciousness.

But unique individuals do not live in a vacuum. We all live and move and have our being in communities. In Whitehead's phrase, the individual is a process immersed in a larger process—and there is no definite line where the community leaves off and the individual begins. From a historical perspective, an individual is an animated focal point of traits resident in a community that transcends him in both space and time. An absolutely unique element or trait would be meaningless. It is the pattern that these traits take in an individual, not the elements that make up the pattern, that defines his uniqueness. The difference between individuals is a matter of the distribution and size of common traits, as is obvious when we are speaking of physical features.

This suggests that if we are to understand an individual's unique personhood (even our own), it is necessary to study the complex of traits that make up *his* community. As the ancient wisdom would have it, "you who pursue deliverance" must "look to the rock from which you were hewn, and to the quarry from which you were digged."[5]

This seems to me what Erik Erikson was arguing when he said that "the term identity points to an individual's link with the unique values, fostered by a unique history of his people."[6] A primary connotation of the term "identity" is that of "a persistent sharing of some kind of essential character with others"—the maintenance of an inner solidarity with a group. Without this sense of solidarity—of belonging—the individual has no roots, no past, and therefore no future. As we say, he feels estranged—separated from others—

and the passing events are experienced as a series of unrelated "happenings."

I suppose that this general view of the nature of "identity" is familiar enough, and that you will grant it "for substance thereof."

The next thing to be noted is that probably the primary fact about our modern world society—wherein it differs most from preceding societies in Christendom—is that it is not tribal[7] but pluralistic. Each of us, by virtue of living in modern society, is conscious of belonging to several more or less coherent and concentric groups—for example, family, church, gang, student body, faculty, university, ethnic group, state, nation, Western civilization, Christendom, humankind, the animal kingdom, the universe. In this situation, if an individual's sense of personal identity is rooted in a feeling of solidarity with a group, the pressing question is, "Which group?" Pluralism means that each person has to answer this question for himself and that each group solicits his choice in the highly competitive market of possibilities. As sociologists tell us, we live in a society that is characterized by "consumer orientation" even in intellectual and spiritual matters. I quote, for example, Thomas Luckmann's *The Invisible Religion*:

> To an immeasurably higher degree than in a traditional social order, the individual is left to his own devices in choosing goods and services, friends, marriage partners, neighbors, hobbies and, as we shall show presently, even "ultimate" meanings in a relatively autonomous fashion. In a manner of speaking, he is free to construct his own personal identity. The consumer orientation, in short, is not limited to economic products but characterizes the relation of the individual to the entire culture. The latter is no longer an obligatory structure of interpretive and evaluative schemes with a distinct hierarchy of significance. It is, rather, a rich, heterogeneous assortment of possibilities which, in principle, are accessible to any individual consumer. It goes without saying that the consumer preferences still remain a function of the consumer's social biography.[8]

In Luckmann's words, every person in our pluralistic society, "in a manner of speaking . . . is free to construct his own personal identity." I would prefer to make the statement even stronger—that in the modern consumer-oriented pluralistic society he *must* choose "his own personal identity,"[9] which, in the context suggested above, is to say that he must choose a mythical or historical community in which to find his identity. It is recognized, to be sure, that the choice is "a function of the consumer's social biography," and circumscribed thereby. But the individual is likely to be unaware of how his choice is conditioned by his biography.[10] What he senses and feels is that the consumer market appears to offer innumerable possibilities and that he must choose.[11] This is what strikes and paralyzes a number of the most able students during their junior and / or senior years in the university. It is the "terrible freedom" of modern man.

Erikson quotes George Bernard Shaw's autobiographical account of his search for and achievement of "identity"—an account that illuminates the situation of Mr. Everyman in our pluralistic society. Shaw's childhood background was extraordinarily fragmented into diverse elements. He was not conscious of being firmly rooted in family, or church, or Ireland, or England. As he put it, he felt

> a deeper strangeness which has made me all my life a sojourner on this planet rather than a native of it. Whether it be that I was born mad or a little too sane, my kingdom was not of this world: I was at home only in the realm of my imagination, and at ease only with the mighty dead.[12]

Being thus estranged, but also being unusually gifted, he found that he

> had to become an actor, and create for myself a fantastic personality . . . adaptable to the various parts I had to play as author, journalist, orator, politician, committee man, man of the world, and so forth.[13]

The fact that he was conscious of playing several roles in society made him conscious that "who he really was" was not contained in any one of them. Noting that he was playing several parts *as an actor*,[14] he realized he was in danger of losing, or of never achieving, any sense of his individual or unique personal identity. What was lacking was a perspective that transcended and included all the roles. As Shaw himself put it, the parts for the construction of an identity were present and "needed only a clear comprehension of life in the light of an intelligible theory; in short a religion, to set it in triumphant operation."[15] This suggests, in keeping with Luckmann's theory, the *choice* of "a religion."

As I understand it, I accept Shaw's definition of "religion" as whatever it is that gives one the feeling that he has "a clear comprehension of life in the light of an intelligible theory." And it seems to me that in our pluralistic society survival in health demands that one make such a choice, either consciously or by default. Without some such intellectually acceptable and emotionally satisfying "clear comprehension of life," living becomes the passive experiencing of disconnected "happenings"—as to Sammy in William Golding's *Free Fall*,[16] who, as an adult, could see or feel no continuity with "the boy" he presumably once was. Shaw's "kingdom was not of this world." His "religion" was the imaginative discovery of a community that transcended all the communities in which he played a part as "an actor"—in time (it included the "mighty dead") and space.

Shaw's experience suggests that stable identity in our pluralistic society depends upon a feeling of "inner solidarity" with a "community" which one *believes* transcends in time and space all the many groups and roles to which he is exposed or belongs.

I suppose that traditionally in Christendom this transcendent community was represented by "the Church," which was not only an abstract theological concept of oneness "in Christ" (as it has become in our modern pluralistic world), but also a tangible and powerful institution with authority in society. To the modern (or secular) person from whose consciousness the

"invisible world" has faded, the phrase "the Church" seems purely emotive—
that is, it points to nothing sensible; but saying it can make some persons feel
the moist herd warmth of a community not of this world.

In the pluralistic United States, with more than 1,000 different organized
religious groups, each offering in the competitive market its peculiar brand of
"salvation," it is almost impossible for a reasonable person to think of his
local church or denomination—or even of an imagined cartel of
denominations with several million members—as relating him to such a
transcendent community. His largely desacralized and profane "church" is
but one organization among many others, and affiliation with it, or
acceptance of its ideology, is a matter of taste.[17] Further, respect for it is
lessened by recognition that it is a highly competitive organization which
exists, as does its contemporary business corporations, to "sell" its product—
the gospel it manufactures out of the common raw materials provided by
Scripture and history. And, in doing so, it will adopt and adapt all the
available technical means for image creation and packaging that its leaders'
abilities and resources make possible.

Any one "church" in our society is too small, too circumscribed in time
and space, too droopy in its thinking, too competitive, too involved in its own
survival, to offer a plausible claim even to point to the transcendent
community necessary for the achievement of the kind of identity of which
Shaw spoke. On the contrary, membership in it imposes on a person the
necessity to play another role as "an actor" in the pluralistic society. From the
perspective of what is accepted as modern knowledge and taught, however
badly, in our schools, Christianity as "a religion" incarnated in the
denominations has become pathetically parochial and provincial—at least in
time, if less so in space.[18]

When Bishop Ussher (1581–1625) did his work during the first quarter of
the seventeenth century, perhaps 1,600 years of Christianity seemed a very
long time, and the almost 6,000 years since creation that he postulated were
perhaps beyond the imagination of most people. But these stretches of time
seem puny indeed in the context of the hypothesis of four billion years before
the emergence of man, and the two or three millions of years postulated for the
aggressive toolmaker's pilgrimage upon the planet, trailing clouds of
pollution behind him. Church historians and theologians with their 2,000
years of subject matter have been compared with one who would take up a
1,000-page volume, read the last sentence, and call it "history."[19] From the
"modern" perspective (and it does not matter whether it is true or false—all
that matters is that it now has the compulsive power of being generally
accepted, which Christianity has lost), organized Christianity is no longer
providing for its members a relation to the kind of transcendent community
necessary for the achievement of stable identity. That this is sensed by many
theological school professors and ministers is suggested by the frenetic quality
of much of their writing and activity,[20] their scrambling after fads,[21] their

bandwagon complex, and the phenomenal exodus from their ranks into "relevant" work.[22]

Apparently, even to many who stay in them, the institutional churches are no longer the residence of the kind of "religion" Shaw was talking about, and their traditional claims are being smothered under the clergy's belated recognition that, in the words of Lincoln, "the dogmas of the quiet past are inadequate to the stormy present . . . [and] as our case is new, so we must think anew and act anew"[23]—something that is relatively impossible in an institution which professes to adhere to the principle that all the wisdom possible for man is concentrated in one moment of his history.[24]

If one grants the conception of "identity" adumbrated above, it seems to follow that, by and large, the larger, the more massive, inclusive, and persistent in time, is the "community" to which one relates—in brief, the more it transcends all the vicissitudes of man's day-by-day experiences—the stronger and more stable will be his sense of personal identity. And, it seems to me, the shape of such a community has been persuasively sketched in the writings of several imaginative scientists, philosophers, journalists, and even some theologians, who collectively seem to constitute the most conscientiously unimaginative professional group in our society.

I cannot as yet project a full-blown picture of that community, and the glimpse of it I can give you will have to be in the form of a personal testimony regarding where and how I think I found it. Because some of you will be skeptical that anything of religious significance could be found there, reminiscent of Phillip's answer to the Nathanael who doubted that "any good thing [could] come out of Nazareth," I can say only, "come and see."[25] You will recognize that in professional lingo this means that I am going to give you a reading list.

Perhaps some will see my perspective as "Christian"—which is to say with theologian Gregory Baum, "that what I [have] said in a new language could be translated back into orthodox talk."[26] This effort, Baum concluded, was his great mistake, for "we do not need the words of scripture and creed to speak about the sickness from which we suffer and the newness offered us."[27] If my perspective can be "translated back into orthodox talk," I leave that task to those who irritated Ralph Waldo Emerson by their inability to recognize and credit virtue unless it bore *their* Christian tag. Such Christians remind me of those who today are spending thousands of dollars to convince me that when I am out of Schlitz I am out of beer.

Bertrand Russell was reaching for the truly transcendent community when his *Education and the Social Order* was published in 1932; in it he concluded that "if our scientific civilization is to survive," it will be necessary for our educational systems to contribute to "international cohesion" by inculcating "a sense of the whole human race as one co-operative unit."[28] Russell used the word "science" in a very inclusive sense to designate a way of thinking that, one might say, was to him "the new Messiah." Although he said he detested all "orthodoxy" as the "grave of intelligence, no matter what orthodoxy it may be,"[29] by implication he made his conception of "scientific thinking" an "orthodoxy." It follows that his conception of "our scientific civilization" was for him an ultimate—the most inclusive community he could conceive of wherein to find his identity.

Now, thirty-eight years later when ecology has become a religion—or a religious fad—and when Roman Catholic freshman girls soberly tell me that the end of the human world is very near, it should be obvious that Russell's community, although it included "the whole human race," is not inclusive enough or secure enough to guarantee one a stable and secure identity. The "modern's" analogy to the traditional "city of God," wherein "neither moth nor rust doth corrupt, and where thieves do not break through nor steal,"[30] is reared on the presupposition of unbroken continuity in the universe through billions of years, and must include not only all "living" things but all "inorganic" matter as well.

Where shall we look for such a community? I have found it in the writings of Loren Eiseley (*The Immense Journey, The Unexpected Universe*), Albert Schweitzer (*Out of My Life and Thought*), Alfred North Whitehead (*Adventures of Ideas*, pts. 1,2; *Modes of Thought*; *The Aims of Education*), Teilhard de Chardin (*The Future of Man, The Phenomenon of Man*), L. Charles Birch (*Nature and God*), and Dorothy Sayers (*The Mind of the Maker*). The list could legitimately be extended almost endlessly, but these are the writings I have found most fruitful. They have one thing in common—of all of them it might be said what one interpreter said of Whitehead's "philosophical position"—it "is not so much the *conclusion* of a philosophical *argument* as an *imaginative construction*."[31] This strikes me as right, for I suppose that we are never going to get to heaven with such a rational structure as the Tower of Babel.

This "imaginative construction" satisfies Shaw's need for a "comprehension of life in the light of an intelligible theory"—"intelligible" because admittedly "scientific," embarrassing as this may be to science. For

> after having chided the theologian for his reliance on myth and miracle, science found itself in the unenviable position of having to create a mythology of its own: namely, the assumption that what, after long effort, could not be proved to take place today had, in truth, taken place in the primeval past.[32]

The myth of origins, yes, but also the mythology of "the beautiful pulse of streaming protoplasm, that unknown organization of an unstable chemistry that makes up the life process,"[33] ". . . life reaching out, groping for a billion years, life desperate to go home."[34] To modify Loren Eiseley's sentence somewhat: We are "projections out of . . . [a] timeless ferment . . . locked . . . in some" incalculable unity with all the past. Man is life conscious of itself. So any man might say, "In many a fin and reptile foot I have seen myself passing by—some part of myself, that is, some part that lies unrealized in the momentary shape I [now] inhabit."[35] And as I looked into the sightless sockets of the fossil being "not a man," I knew that this "creature had never lived to see a man, and I [wondered], what was it I was never going to see?"[36]

This is all a part of the mythology of "modern" man—a dimension of the "invisible environment" which lies "not so much in his surroundings as in man's brain, in his way of looking at the world around him and at the social environment he was beginning to create."[37] This "invisible environment" peopled with "the unseen gods [that] . . . stalk through his dreams" is the reward, or penalty, attached to consciousness. And consciousness, which is life becoming aware of itself, is a most fragile thing—"a few moments' loss of vital air and the phenomenon. . . goes down into the black night of inorganic things."[38] While contemplation of this fragility is an ever-present source of terror, it is also a constant reminder of the unbroken continuity of the living and the inorganic, which was caught in the ancient celebration of the great "Thou–I" cycle, "dust thou art, to dust returnest," but only to return again as an "I."

Finally, I am trying to suggest that the "modern" can find a stable identity only in the context of unimaginable time, as he senses a mystical unity with all of life on its "immense journey." This is the passionate imaginative recognition of unbroken continuity in the physical universe, and in all of life in its manifold forms and monstrous shapes—the staggering awareness that we *are* life, life at last become aware of itself and henceforth burdened with the awful responsibility for its destiny in the universe.

Loren Eiseley has most vividly communicated to me this sense of being not "man" but "life." We ask, as a child asks his mother,

"Where did I come from?" "Son," you say floundering, "below the Cambrian there was a worm." Or you say, "There was an odd fish in a swamp and you have his lungs." Or you say, "Once there was a reptile whose jaw bones are in your ear." Or you try again, "There was an ape and his teeth are in your mouth. . . . You are fish and reptile and a warm-blooded, affectionate thing that dies if it has nothing to cling to when it is young. You are also a rag doll made of patches out of many ages and skins. You began nowhere in particular. You are really an illusion, one of innumerable shadows in the dying fires of a mysterious universe. Yesterday you were a lowbrowed skull in the river gravel; tomorrow you may be a fleck of carbon amid the shattered glass of Moscow or New York." Ninety percent of the world's life has already gone. Perhaps brains will accomplish the work of extinction more rapidly. The pace is stepping up.[39]

But meanwhile, I know I

have slept in wood nests and hissed in the uncouth guise of waddling amphibians. [And] we have played such roles for infinitely longer ages than we have been men. Our identity is a dream. We are process, not reality, for reality is an illusion of the daylight—the light of our particular day. In a fortnight, as aeons are measured, we may lie silent in a bed of stone, or, as has happened in the past, be figured in another guise.[40]

We find a stable identity only through an imaginative grasp that we are one with all of life in time and space, and, recognizing that there is no marked

boundary between what we call organic or inorganic, that human life *is* the
planet become conscious of itself. It is a planet in travail, and there is no good
reason for supposing that man is the final birth.[41] All that can be said is that he
seems, with the fearful measure of control he has achieved, to be responsible
for the future of his world. Meantime the purpose of the study of history
should be to orient the individual to this great community, oneness with which
Loren Eiseley so persuasively presents:

> Imagine, for a moment, that you have drunk from a magician's goblet. Reverse the
> irreversible stream of time. Go down the dark stairwell out of which the race has
> ascended. Find yourself at last on the bottommost steps of time, slipping, sliding, and
> wallowing by scale and fin down into the muck and ooze out of which you arose. Pass by
> grunts and voiceless hissings below the last tree ferns. Eyeless and earless, float in the
> primal waters, sense sunlight you cannot see and stretch absorbing tentacles toward
> vague tastes that float in water. Still, in your formless shiftings, the *you* remains: the
> sliding particles, the juices, the transformations are working in an exquisitely patterned
> rhythm which has no other purpose than your preservation—you, the entity, the
> ameboid being whose substance contains the unfathomable future.[42]

[1]This paper was presented at the American Society of Church History meeting, April 24, 1970,
at the University of Iowa, and was subsequently published in *The Journal of Religion*, XI
(January, 1971), 1–14.

[2]Loren Eiseley, *The Immense Journey*, Time Reading Program Special Edition (New York:
Time Inc., 1962), pp. 90–91.

[3]Compare Neil Postman and Charles Weingartner, *Teaching as a Subversive Activity* (New
York: Delacorte Press, 1969).

[4]Compare the following: "Process philosophy sees 'personal identity' as an abstraction: it is
the element of permanence in the series of momentary selves which together constitute a
'person'—*but it has no existence apart from that series.* Since human 'personal identity' or
'personality' are widely regarded as modern equivalents to the word 'soul,' this last statement
strikes at the very roots of the idea of the immortality of the human soul—an idea that by no
means coincides with the biblical doctrine of resurrection, but is none the less one of the most
cherished beliefs of many Christians, whilst also acting as a major stumbling-block to the faith of
many 'modern men.'" Peter Hamilton, *The Living God and the Modern World: Christian
Theology Based on the Thought of A. N. Whitehead* (Philadelphia: United Church Press, 1969),
pp. 28–29.

[5]Isaiah 51:1, RSV.

[6]Erik H. Erikson, "The Problem of Ego Identity," in *Identity and Anxiety*, ed. Maurice R.
Stein *et al.* (Glencoe, IL: Free Press, 1960), p. 38. "The sense of ego identity, then, becomes more
necessary (and more problematical) wherever a wide range of possible identities is envisaged.
Identity is a term used in our day with faddish ease; at this point, I can only indicate how very
complicated the real article is. For ego identity is partially conscious and largely unconscious. It is
a psychological process reflecting social processes; but with sociological means it can be seen as a
social process reflecting psychological processes; it meets its crisis in adolescence, but has grown
through childhood and continues to reemerge in the crises of later years. The overriding meaning

of it all, then, is the creation of a sense of sameness, a unity of personality now felt by the individual and recognized by others as having consistency in time—of being, as it were, an irreversible historical fact." Erik H. Erikson, "Youth, Fidelity and Diversity," in *The Challenge of Youth*, ed. Erik H. Erikson (Garden City, NY: Doubleday & Co., 1965), p. 13.

[7]See Henry Bamford Parkes, *Gods and Men: The Origins of Modern Culture* (New York: Random House, 1965), pp. 8–15.

[8](New York: Macmillan Co., 1967), p. 98.

[9]Compare Postman and Weingartner, p. 11: "But now, in just the last minute, we've reached the stage where change occurs so rapidly that each of us in the course of our lives has continuously to work out a set of values, beliefs, and patterns of behavior that are viable, or *seem* viable, to each of us personally. And just when we have identified a workable system, it turns out to be irrelevant because so much had changed while we were doing it."

[10]For example, Bertrand Russell, who intellectually and consciously "chose" the Greek way, found that he *felt* at home in Greece only when he went into the small Byzantine church. *Autobiography* (New York: Simon & Schuster, 1969), 3:84–85. And Will Durant: "though the dogmas of the old faith have gone from me . . . they have left in me an aroma of their memory." *On the Meaning of Life* (New York: Ray Long & Richard R. Smith, 1932), p. 132.

[11]"From his point of view" the individual "is working within a frame of choice, not of destiny." And it is "the way a man defines his situation [that] constitutes for him its reality. Choice for him is a paramount fact; how matters appear to the watcher on the hill is [for him] irrelevant." Mary Ellen Goodman, *The Individual and Culture* (Homewood, IL: Dorsey Press, 1967), p. 7.

[12]"The Problem of Ego Identity," Erik Erikson, in *Identity and Anxiety*, ed. by Maurice R. Stein *et al.* (Glencoe, IL: Free Press, 1960), p. 44.

[13]*Ibid.*

[14]See Erving Goffmann, *The Presentation of the Self in Everyday Life* (New York: Doubleday & Co., 1959), *passim.*

[15]Erikson, "The Problem of Ego Identity," p. 44.

[16]New York: Harcourt, Brace and World, Inc., 1951, *passim.*

[17]Note, for example, that clergyman of the Evangelical Alliance who argued in 1846 that the Christian must join a denomination because he must belong to the church visible as well as invisible. But henceforth, he added, let his choice of a denomination be a matter of preference, not of exclusion. It was a notable thing in Christian history when modes of baptism, forms of church polity, etc., ceased to be defended on the basis of scriptural authority. *Evangelical Alliance: Report of the Proceedings of the Conference, Held at Freemasons Hall, London, from August 19 to September 2 Inclusive, 1846* (London: Partridge & Oakey, 1847), p. 87.

[18]A denomination in the pluralistic United States might be seen as a subculture as defined by some anthropologists, for example, Goodman, p. 37.

[19]Compare the familiar metaphor of a clock face, as used, for example, by Postman and Weingartner, pp. 10–11.

[20]Charles R. Feilding, who directed a very extensive study of education for ministry, concluded that "the greater part of the whole theological enterprise seems . . . to be off on a vast archaeological dig, preoccupied with the long ago and largely oblivious of the purpose of the expedition" (*Education for Ministry* [Dayton, OH: American Association of Theological Schools, 1966], p. 10.) With this in mind, what Postman and Weingartner (p. 13) say about teachers could as well be applied to clergymen in general, and to theological school professors in particular: "Most teachers have the idea that they are in some sort of business. . . The signs that their business is failing are abundant, but they keep at it all the more diligently. Santayana told us that a fanatic is someone who redoubles his efforts when he has forgotten his aim. In this case, even if the aim has not been forgotten, it is simply irrelevant. But the effort has been redoubled anyway." That the effort seems to have been redoubled is suggested by the advertisements for the seminaries and the theological schools in the *Christian Century*, April 22, 1970. This is the issue devoted to "Theological Education 1970."

[21]See, for example, Michael Novak, in "Spring Book Report," *National Catholic Reporter*, April 17, 1970, p. 7: "There are many fads. . . . The theology of the future is a fad, the theology of celebration is a fad. The dialogue between Marxism and Christianity is a fad. The sudden discovery by religious people of the social sciences . . . is also a fad. I mean by 'fad' that many people are putting more weight upon these various directions than they will bear; and rather (?) soon there will be a restless herd seeking other pastures."

[22]It is a notable event when a nonprofit Career Programming Institute is set up "to assist clergymen of all denominations who are transferring out of the active ministry to make a personally successful transfer to secular employment," and said institute manages to survive on the relatively small tuition fee it charges (see ibid., pp. 1, 20).

[23]Philip Van Doren Stern, ed., *The Life and Writings of Abraham Lincoln* (New York: Modern Library, 1940), p. 745.

[24]The modern theme is continuity—"that life emerged or evolved from non-life without the addition of 'something extra' from 'outside' [creation]." There is no sharp discontinuity between living and nonliving material. All this is apt to shock the Christian. He "will be protected against this 'shock' if he has come to think of the entire history of this planet as one continuous process of evolution from the time it spun off from the sun to the present day (and beyond), and see God's love as operative throughout this entire process, not concentrated at certain key points. Teilhard de Chardin offers us a vision of this in *The Phenomenon of Man* and A. N. Whitehead and Charles Hartshorne attempt an analysis as to *how* God's love is operative" (Hamilton, p. 43).

[25]John I:43–46.

[26]In "Spring Book Report," *National Catholic Reporter*, April 17, 1970, p. 7.

[27]*Ibid.*

[28](London: George Allen & Unwin, 1932), p. 27.

[29]*Ibid.*, p. 21.

[30]Matthew 6:20.

[31]Hamilton, p. 25, quoting V. C. Chappell, who argued that this is what made " 'Whitehead's later work uninteresting at best to many contemporary philosophers,' for whom philosophy is basically argumentative." Horace Bushnell might be said to have anticipated this approach in his sermon, "Our Gospel a Gift to the Imagination" [1869], in *Building Eras in Religion* (New York: Charles Scribner's Sons, 1910), pp. 249–85. The significance of imagination has its defenders today, for example, Benjamin DeMott, *Supergrow: Essays and Reports on Imagination in America* (New York: E. P. Dutton & Co., 1969).

[32]Eiseley, *The Immense Journey*, p. 144.

[33]*Ibid.*, p. 32.

[34]*Ibid.*, p. 31.

[35]*Ibid.*, p. 17.

[36]*Ibid.*, pp. 2–3.

[37]*Ibid.*, p. 87.

[38]Loren Eiseley, *The Unexpected Universe* (New York: Harcourt, Brace & World, 1969), p. 52.

[39]Loren Eiseley, "The Time of Man," in *The Light of the Past: A Treasury of Horizon* (New York: American Heritage Publishing Co., 1965), p. 38.

[40]Eiseley, *The Unexpected Universe*, p. 76.

[41]It has been suggested that man appears to be the missing link between anthropoid apes and human beings.

[42]*The Immense Journey*, p. 147.

II CHURCH HISTORY EXPLAINED[1]

History and church history are disciplines well entrenched in the schools. This means that church historians commonly have an unquestioned place in theological school faculties. Hence there is little incentive for them to become self-conscious or troubled about the reason-for-being either of the discipline or of themselves. Probably church history is always included in the curriculum more from habit than because there is an articulated rationale for it. I dare say that many church historians if asked the question, "Why have church history in the curriculum?" would reply in effect that its place is obvious, and if one cannot see the obvious it is hopeless to try to explain it to him.

But, as Charles A. Beard once said, "Even the historian would be a strange creature if he never asked himself why he regarded these matters as worthy of his labor and love, or why society provides a living for him during his excursions and explorations."[2] I am not *that* strange, so I have asked myself those questions and pondered possible answers. What follows is my present formulation of my view of what church history is. Perhaps its presentation will suggest an answer to the question, "Why have it in the curriculum?"

One's answer to the question will of course be conditioned by his opinion of (1) the nature of the history of the historians both as to content and method; (2) how the peculiar nature of "church" history is to be defined— e.g., is it a peculiarity only of content, or is there also a peculiarity of approach; (3) of the purpose of a theological school which exists primarily for the education and training of parish ministers; and (4) the best possible curriculum to achieve this primary aim.

Below I shall concentrate on the nature of the history of the historians, and on how the peculiar nature of church history may be conceived. My views are of course affected by the peculiarities of my professional experience. I have worked exclusively in what is called "American church history" which today is oriented more in general American history than in church history— and one is not only known but conditioned by the company he keeps. Further, I have always taught in an interdenominational situation, which makes me the servant of all, subject to the scrutiny of all. This accounts for what irritated particularists have called my expertness in chameleonship.

In our society the university is the arbiter of learning and definer of the branches of knowledge. The branches of knowledge receive recognition as *disciplines* in the university by being organized into semi-autonomous departments—often staffed by semi-autonomous prima donnas. The one-time chancellor of The University of Chicago defined the university as an "agglomeration of entities connected only by a central heating system." A former president of the University of California at Berkeley has defined a university faculty as a group of "independent entrepreneurs held together by a common grievance over parking!"[3]

Be that as it may—and is—history is one of the recognized disciplines of the university with such departmental status and some such characters.

I assume that one's intellectual quest, if it is to be effective, must take place—or at least begin—within one or more of the existing disciplines, usually, but not necessarily, in a university. As university organization proliferates and increasingly dominates study we more and more face the danger that we will conventionalize knowledge, and sterilize education, by organizing it in such fashion that individuals may acquire a personal vested interest in perpetuating its existing but outmoded forms. Every professor with tenure and every administrator bears constant watching as a potential menace to the continued advancement of learning.

I also assume that whatever church history may be, if church historians are to remain in the great conversation which characterizes the historical discipline, they must remain in dialogue with those in the university's departments of history. It follows that the church historian's view of the nature of written history must be recognizable as valid by at least a significant number of general historians. Therefore I shall speak first of the nature of the historian's history in a fashion that most professional historians will grant is an acceptable view though it is not theirs.

History originates in curiosity about the past. Where there is no such curiosity there can be no historical quest, and little appreciation of the nature of historical studies and their place in a curriculum. To make a plea for history before such an audience would be an example of casting pearls before swine.

Where such curiosity exists it is manifested in questions. The type question is, "How did this present come to be out of that past?"—or, if you wish, "How did I, or we, or they, get *that* way?" The first step to understanding any written history is to ascertain what question the author intended to answer. Book reviewers who do not begin here commonly criticize an author for not writing the kind of book the reviewer thinks he would have written. Because the questions of a period grow out of that period's interests, the questions asked by historians change with changing times. The history written in one era may not interest the people of a following era because they are no longer interested in the same questions. And in history as elsewhere, nothing is as useless as the answer to an unasked question. This suggests a basic reason why histories have continually to be rewritten. It also suggests that the reason why some courses in history seem dull to the students is that they are not interested in the questions the professor is answering. Half the job in teaching history is in getting the students interested in the questions the professor deems important.

Commonly there is a practical reason for the questions. People want to know how they "got that way" in order to understand their present situation in such fashion as to suggest what they can and ought to do. As Carl Becker said, the "natural function of history" is to enable us to judge what we are doing "in light of what we have done and what we hope to do." Ralph Barton Perry stated it as the attempt "to conceive the thought of the past as truly as possible, and to connect it with the future through present analysis and appraisal." In this respect Abraham Lincoln is my ideal type of historian. He began the so-called "House Divided" speech with the remark, "If we could first know where we are, and whither we are tending, we could better judge what to do, and how to do it." He then proceeded to an acute historical analysis of the immediate past in such fashion as to suggest where they then were and whither tending. And when this was persuasively presented, what they should do and how they should do it was clear. Jefferson, too, spoke in this vein when he argued that history ought to be included in the curriculum of the university because "History, by appraizing. . . . [the students] of the past, will enable them to judge of the future."

The corollary of what I have said is that every written history is essentially an assertion in the form of a thesis that constitutes an answer to a question about the past. The totality of such assertions constitutes the body of historical knowledge.

These assertions are made about three things.

First (only in order of mention) are assertions about the activities of people done in the past—about what people did and when and where they did it—for example, "Columbus sailed the ocean blue in fourteen-hundred-and-ninety-two."

Second are assertions about "ideology"—where the word "ideology" merely points to the content and way of thinking that characterizes an individual, or a group, or an era. These assertions about what the individual or group being studied thought he or they were doing are based upon inferences from what they said, and / or the artifacts they left. The actions of people are explained by pointing to the motives that lie back of them. The study of what people said they thought they were doing is the study of their conception of why they were doing it as they did—that is, of their motives. The ascertainment of motives is a chief goal of historical studies because our understanding of the people of the past depends upon our understanding of what motivated them. What the historian thinks motivated people is rooted in his conception of the nature of man. This consideration is very important in understanding the nature of historical interpretation.

Third are assertions about unquestioned presuppositions. A study of characteristic contents and ways of thinking leads always to presuppositions that lie behind the whole ideological structure. These are harder to get at than matters of ideology because, being assumed, they are seldom self-consciously defined and articulated. They are "obvious," and the statement of the obvious is one of the most difficult of intellectual achievements. But one never fully understands a person or a group until and unless one understands what he or they assume or presuppose and why they do so. To quote H. Richard Niebuhr,

> no movement can be understood until its presuppositions, the fundamental faith upon which it rests, have been at least provisionally adopted. The presuppositions may not be our own; we may find good reason for rejecting them in favor of others; but we cannot understand without occupying a standpoint, and there is no greater barrier to understanding than the assumption that the standpoint which we happen to occupy is a universal one, while that of the object of our criticism is relative.[4]

The historian makes assertions about these three aspects of human life—activities, ideology, presuppositions—in answer to the questions: What did they do? When and where did they do it? What did they think they were doing and why? What did they presuppose?

His context is the discipline of history which defines his method or approach. His method has two aspects.

First is the aspect of what are called "facts." The foundation of all historical work is the establishment of "facts." Granted the discipline of history, all acceptable historical knowledge consists in that which meets with the consensus of those trained to be in a position to judge when a "fact" has been established. This is to recognize the place of the specialist who has paid the price of disciplined study. A specialist will be acutely aware of the limitations of his knowledge. Hence he may appear to be at a disadvantage when confronted with the critic of his findings—as he not infrequently is—who says in effect, "I do not know much about this period, but it seems to me. . . ." A New England minister gave the specialists a ready-made answer when he told such a critic, I cannot permit your ignorance, however vast, to take precedence over my knowledge, however limited.

The historian's "facts" have their peculiar character. The assertions about activities, ideology, and presuppositions which make up the sum of historical knowledge, are to be seen on a continuum. At one end, let us say the left, are those assertions upon which there is no consensus whatsoever. At the other end are those assertions upon which there is complete consensus.

Commonly when we refer to "facts" we have in mind those assertions that lie well toward the right end of the continuum. But we must keep in mind that there are no matters forever settled and beyond question in historical knowledge. There is no finality about any of the assertions. This is to say that so far as the nature of the knowing is concerned there is no fence separating an area of settled "facts" from an area of "interpretations." So far as the way of knowing is concerned, historical knowledge is all of a piece whether one is talking about *when* Lincoln was born or *why* Booth shot him. It is all based on inferences from "remains," or, if you prefer, the interpretation of sources.

The second aspect of the historian's method is that of interpretation. An interpretation is an assertion about some aspect of the past stated in terminology meaningful to the historian's contemporary audience. Insofar as the historian's worldview differs from the worldview of the people being studied, an interpretation is a translation of a past ideology into contemporary ideology. For example we refer to dates "B.C."

Granted the desirability of maintaining a sense of continuity with the past—and this is a necessary presupposition for historical work—it is maintained by interpreting the past in such fashion that it can be sympathetically understood and appropriated by contemporary minds. Whatever in the past cannot thus be translated into contemporary ideology can be no part of contemporary historical knowledge. Hence the historian at difficult points is always tempted literally to *create* a past. This is sometimes called "conjectural interpolation."

Interpretation of course takes place in a modern mind, characterized by presuppositions and ideology largely absorbed from the dynamic community in which that mind has been nurtured. Primarily here is a conception of the final outcome or end of the story. As A. N. Whitehead said,

> The historian in his description of the past depends on his own judgment as to what constitutes the importance of human life. Even when he has vigorously confined himself to one selected aspect, political or cultural, he still depends on some decision as to what constitutes the culmination of that phase of human experience and as to what constitutes its degradation.[5]

Thus the historian's value orientation directly conditions his historiography—something some historians have been reluctant to admit—by giving him a selective principle. He picks from the past what will bring his story to the culmination to which he is committed.

The historian is selective in another sense. A history cannot be a description of every detail of all the past or of any small part thereof—even one hour. One of the canons of the historians is that

> every written history . . . is a selection of facts made by some person or persons and is ordered or organized under the influence of some scheme of reference, interest, or emphasis . . . in the thought of the author or authors.[6]

The historian's selection of what to emphasize in the past depends upon his conception of the end and culmination of the story he wishes to tell—which story is itself selected from a practically infinite number of possible stories. A comparison of the histories of religious or political developments in America will make this clear.

When the story being told comes down to the historian's present the culmination of his story must be an imaginative projection into the future—his conception of the shape of things to come. As has been said, "What is basic in that history involves a reference to its predicted outcome." But what is found in the present "is not yet fully worked out. Rather, the present suggests what will eventuate in time to come. Thus we understand what is basic in a history in terms of some . . . 'present tendency' directed toward the future."[7]

Because "the present is full of such tendencies, it suggests many different possible futures" and different tendencies appeal to different people. "The historian selects one of these possible futures . . . and uses it as a principle by which to select what is basic among the multitude of facts at his disposal."[8]

This selection "necessarily involves a certain choice of allegiance, an act of faith in one kind of future rather than another"—a betting that this particular tendency will prove dominant tomorrow. But because the historian is himself a part of the history-that-happens, "to say that a principle of selection is [thus] 'chosen' does not mean that such choices are arbitrary. Men do not arbitrarily 'choose' their allegiances and faiths, even when they are converts." Rather "their faiths are . . . forced upon them." This is to say that "the history-that-happens itself generates the faiths and allegiances that furnish the principles for selecting what is important in understanding it."[9]

This situation is inherent in the nature of historical knowledge and written history. The historian attempts to note what people did and to explain why they did it. Insofar as he has no explanation there can be no *history* of that event. To say that a choice was "arbitrary" is just another way of saying that it is inexplicable. And what is inexplicable cannot be a part of historical knowledge.

It follows from these considerations that every written history is at least implicitly an explanation and defense of the allegiance—the faith— of the historian. It points to that to which the historian is committed. In this respect the Christian historian does not differ from the non-Christian historians. His conflict with them, if any, is a conflict of allegiances—of faiths—and should be recognized as such. This means that the basic differences between historians—or between schools of historians—are theological and/ or philosophical and cannot be resolved by historical methods. This suggests at least that theology *is* "the Queen of the sciences," the final arbiter between the claims of the several disciplines and between the schools within disciplines.

It also follows from the conception of history I have adumbrated that the historical interpretation of the past by a modern mind is a pushing toward a more and more complete understanding of the forces that have shaped that mind and made it what it is. In this sense the goal of historical study is self-knowledge. I cannot conceive of self-understanding except as an understanding of how we came to be what we are, or of how I got "that way." It is this kind of self-knowledge that to my mind is of the essence of human freedom. For one is about as much the slave of the forces that have shaped him—that is, of his past—as he is ignorant of them—or of it. Only insofar as one is consciously aware of the dynamic forces within the culture in which he has been nurtured, as a fish is in water, is he freed to make intelligent choices regarding them. Indeed, once he has achieved such awareness he is forced to exercise choice. I suppose this is the reason why some have spoken of "terrible freedom." It is terrifying because to be free means to have to make decisions, and the responsibility for making decisions of significance for their own lives or for the lives of others terrifies many people.

Such freedom comes even when the awareness is of those aspects of experience which cannot be controlled or escaped—what Herbert Butterfield calls "the system of necessity" or of Providence within which we live and have our being. It used to be said that you could take the boy out of the country, but you could not take the country out of the boy. Similarly I suppose the born and bred Methodist may take himself out of the Methodist church, but the chances are that the Methodism will never be completely taken out of the man even though his investments turn out well and he becomes a Presbyterian or Episcopalian. Thus at least one aspect of one's freedom is a self-conscious awareness of and reconciled attitude toward those aspects of his self and culture which he cannot escape. This, I take it, is what Margaret Fuller had grasped when she exclaimed, "I accept the universe." And Carlyle was probably not disagreeing with her, but only chiding her for the lateness of this insight in her life, when he snapped, "Gad, she'd better!"

So much for my conception of the nature of the history of the historians and some of the implications of this view.

In this context, how is the unique nature of *church* history to be defined?

Granted the views sketched above, it ought to be anticipated that to my mind the peculiarity of church history is one of content and not of method or approach. As the title implies, the peculiar subject matter is "the Church." This does not mean that the problem is simple because, as Professor James Hastings Nichols once put it, the basic problem for church historians today is "What and where is 'the Church'?" One cannot escape this problem by conceiving of Christianity as a movement and saying he will write of the Christian movement. For "Christian" is no easier to define than "Church"— and anyway the one is inextricably bound up with the other.

How then shall the peculiar subject matter of church history be defined?

It may be defined empirically or practically. Because church history is a well-established discipline the budding church historian is nurtured in the context of a generally accepted or routine definition of its content as exemplified, for example, in the textbooks (in America, especially Williston Walker's). Broadly this includes all the outward, observable, and institutionalized manifestations of the Christian movement in the history-that-happens. The study presumably includes all those individuals and groups that have called themselves, or been called by others, "Christian."

The study must be serious, and begin with the realization that it may affect one's conception of "the Church" and of what is "Christian." The historian cannot begin in a vacuum. He begins with *some* conception of what the Church is (or is not)—probably what scholars disdainfully refer to as "a popular understanding." And as it is the business of education to violate intellectual innocence, so it is the business of disciplined history to correct the misunderstandings and distortions of popular history. It is this serious willingness to accept whatever results, or lack of results, the application of accepted methods yields which constitutes the historian's "objectivity." Objectivity is not disinterested spectatorship in the historian any more than it is in the detective or lawyer. It is acceptance only of what can be "proved" in the court.

But church historians themselves may continue to operate within the context of traditional and popular understandings of the nature of "the Church." *We* have inherited the discipline of church history. Historically the discipline was shaped largely in the European situation which made it plausible to accept an institutional entity called "the Church" and relatively minor entities called "sects" or "dissenters." The difference between them was that the former was considered to be the mainstream of true Christianity and the latter aberrations which if suppressed or ignored long enough would disappear. Hence the traditional categories of church history are "church," "dissenter," "sect,"—"Christian," "heretic," "schismatic."

But the proliferation of religious groups in the modern world, and especially in America under religious freedom, has made absurd any one group's claim to be the only institutionalized incarnation of "the body of Christ." So today the doleful saint of many church historians is Mary Magdalene, and with her they lament, they have taken away my Lord's body and I know not where to find it. It is for this reason that the content of church history has for many become vague and indefinite, while those who tend to solve such problems by "whistling in the dark" have tended to become increasingly narrow and dogmatic in asserting what that content is. A widespread conclusion of the former is clearly stated by William Alva Gifford in his *The Story of the Faith: A Survey of Christian History for the Undogmatic*: "I have described the twentieth century only in terms of forces and tendencies in religious life and thought; for the 'Christian Church' has strictly ceased to exist. In its place are 'churches,' very many of them, and each with a history of its own. This is especially true in the United States. The history of Christianity there is now the history of denominations, to be written in a multitude of monographs. This is not my undertaking."[10]

Mr. Gifford's conclusion is reflected in the way church history is commonly presented in the seminaries of the United States. A survey of church history carries the student down through the Reformation, or perhaps into the seventeenth century. This survey is followed by a course in the history of that denomination's development in America. The implication would seem to be that that denomination is the direct and / or only significant continuation of "the Church" in history, so the several hundred other denominations may safely be ignored.

It is because of this kind of breakdown of the traditional definition of the content of church history that church historians are being prodded into asking questions about the ideal nature and content of their discipline. This means that they are being forced to consider these matters theoretically—as is always the case when a routine breaks down. The practical or empirical definition of content no longer fits the actualities of the situation in which they must do their work. This pushes them into speculation about the relationship between their observed and their conceptual orders.

I suggest the following theoretical considerations.

The church historian works within the context of the whole theological tradition of Christendom. This tradition exemplifies the ways in which Christians have conceived and articulated the meaning of Christianity for Christians, and have tried to explain it to, or defend it against, non-Christians. The study of that tradition is the study of the ideology and presuppositions of the people called "Christian."

The overwhelming consensus of Christians has been and is that "the Church" is one body—that it is a continuous and dynamic organic unity in history. It is, Christians have said, one in the mind and intent of God; it is one in the mystical unity of the individual believers with Christ the head; and it is one in cherishing and perpetuating the faith under the guidance of the Spirit. This is a simple descriptive, historical assertion.

In this context the appealing practical solution suggested by Mr. Gifford is theoretically inadequate and unsatisfactory.

I think the church historian may assert wherein the unity of his subject matter consists in a way that will enable him to remain in the great conversation with the profane historians on the one hand, and the Christian tradition on the other. At least I have not yet been kicked out of the "secular" historians' fraternity, which is perhaps an exemplification of their Christian charity. In fairness I should add that once upon a time an eminent church historian looked me in the eye and declared, "Strictly speaking, there is no *American* church history, is there!"—thus consigning me-as-career to oblivion.

History is thinking about, and the study of, the *meaning* of the past to the historian's present. The historian thinks of meaning in terms of events and their consequences. Hence, for example, we say that as more and more consequences of the decision for religious freedom in the United States unfold in the history-that-happens, we more and more clearly understand the meaning of that event.

I suppose that the central event of church history—as for that matter, of the history of Western civilization—is the career of Jesus of Nazareth. Historically we understand its meaning in terms of its unfolding consequences. Hence theoretically considered, the content of church history has to do with the consequences of the career of Jesus. No self-conscious person in Western civilization can avoid taking some of these consequences into account, even in such a simple act as setting the date for the next committee meeting. Jesus Christ, as Ralph Waldo Emerson said, is plowed into our experience, that is, into the ground the historian cultivates.

The most tangible, ever present, manifestation of these consequences in our American society is the institutions we call denominations. Not only in profession but also in actuality, these are the outstanding observable consequences in our day of the career of Jesus.

However well or adequately these institutions manifest the real or true meaning of Jesus Christ in history is, of course, a moot question. But the only basis for adjudicating this question is itself to be found only in what these institutions have brought to us on the stream of history. The fact that the question inevitably comes suggests that almost everyone thinks there is some guiding or normative standard carried within these institutions that can be invoked. The most common criticism of the churches is that they do not live up to their heritage and profession. But from whence did the critic learn what the profession and heritage are except from the churches?

Here is suggested a theoretical justification for the church historian beginning with a routine view of the content, form, and general structure of church history as defined for him by the discipline. In America he should begin where he is, by studying the denominations as they are.

This is to say that the beginning of the study is neither to identify nor to prove the existence of "the Church" in the history-that-happens, but to assume that it is there all the time. The God of Abraham, Isaac, and Jacob— the Father of the Lord Jesus Christ—is never without His people. To identify it, or them, is a goal, not the starting point of the study. And it seems reasonable to suppose that the application of historical methods to the study of the institutions that throughout all of Christendom's history have claimed, or have been thought to be, "the Church," will result in the pouring into the earthen vessel of the historian's understanding a more excellent conception of what and where the true Church was, and is, and ought to be. In this sense the study of "church" history resolves itself into the study of the meaning of the actual and visible Church—just as the study of the history of the United States resolves into the study of the meaning of the United States in history.

It is this existing "Church" as is that the historian ought to be trying to understand, and to help to a self-understanding of itself by reminding it of how it came to be what it is. Perhaps he can best know what it is in fact if he is a responsible member of it.

What he thinks the Church is from his experience is the beginning point of his study. No one could begin the study either of the Church or of the United States without some conception of their purpose to which he is committed. This is to say that the historian begins with an allegiance to one of perhaps several conceivable ends or culminations of his story of the Church. It is this commitment that provides the unity to his work. Confronted empirically with all the divisions and diversities of the Church (or of the United States), it is only in the projection of an ideal outcome that he can see the diversity as a unified whole. Insofar he cannot escape a consideration of "last things."

This is why it can be said that what one sees as important in the past depends upon what he wills to prevail in the future. Conversely, the surest clue to what a person really wants to prevail in the future is what he thinks is significant in his past. A historian's Church, therefore, is the company of those past and present, dead and living, who have willed and do will to prevail as or what he does. For the Christian the Church is the company of those who have willed with Jesus "Thy kingdom come, Thy will be done, on earth as it is in heaven." Christians have and do differ, not on this but on the meaning of "Thy kingdom come, Thy will be done"—that is, on what is God's will and what is His Kingdom; and on how one knows the will of God; and on how one is able, or enabled, to will that it may be done.

Within this broad context I have my own view of the peculiar nature of the Church in America, and hence of the nature of American church history.

I begin with the statement of a common working hypothesis borrowed from Tillich, that "religion is the substance of culture and culture the form of religion." I then suppose that the religion of which our American culture (insofar as we have one) is the form, is the Jewish-Christian. This supposition is plausible because this culture as such has no pre-Christian past.

It is implied in the hypothesis that all the tangible manifestations of our culture in the flowing robe of events somehow point to their source in that religious tradition. In it we live and move and have our being as "American." Therefore our American minds find no solid foundation for the intellectual quest to understand who and what we are until they are somehow oriented to that tradition.

Thus beginning with the hypothesis that a culture is the form of a religion, and that the religion of which our culture is the form is the Jewish-Christian, the content of my history of that religion in America is potentially inclusive of everything that is or can be known about the origins and development of the American way of life. Theoretically everything is grist for my little mill. Actually in practice, as suggested above, I begin, and sometimes end, with those institutions and individuals commonly recognized as "Christians." But I would always leave the way open to the possibility, for example, that at one juncture of the history the religion was more truly given form in Abraham Lincoln, who claimed and was claimed by no existing denomination, than by any institution then or now commonly called "Christian." I would do this for the same reason—as I understand it—that Jesus told some of the churchmen of his day that the prostitutes and tax-collectors would enter into the Kingdom of God before them.

In the discussion of history above, I noted the place of presuppositions. In the present context, the presuppositions of our American culture have to do with the Jewish-Christian view of the existence and nature of God; the nature and structure of the universe; and the nature and destiny of man. Therefore, one of the surest clues to the presuppositions on which the ideological structure of our culture is built is to be found in the systematic theologies, the creeds and confessions of our churches. For example, all the creeds assert "I (or we) believe in God." What does this mean intellectually? I think it means, on the one hand, that we presuppose in all our thinking that God exists—that is, that we presuppose in all our thinking that there is order and purpose in the universe ascertainable in part and one way or another by man. On the other hand it means that we presuppose that the universe does not exist absolutely but is contingent—which is to say that Christians do not worship the universe, or America, or anything created, but only God the creator.

There is a sense in which we discover order through our intellectual efforts. But our intellectual quest itself was launched from the hypothesis that there is order to be discovered and used, that is, with belief in God.

Further, all the creeds assert belief in the incarnation—that is, that God assumed human form in history in the being who was very God and very man. Assuming that God is eternal, this means, to me, that once in history, God is always in history. Hence the study of the history-that-happens is always somehow the study of the works of God in history—and by his works we shall know Him, though now we see only through a glass darkly. The perceptive historian sees what Whitehead called "the eternal greatness incarnate in the passage of temporal fact." And in this sense church history is a continuous meditation on the meaning of the incarnation.

Because these matters may either be apprehended and accepted by faith and celebrated in worship, or presupposed as the foundation for the intellectual quest, they ideally bind faith and reason together inextricably. In an integrated Christian civilization the faithful worship of God in the churches would be a declaration of the primary presuppositions that are the foundations of its intellectual life, and the sacrament would be a constant reminder that God is eternally ever-present among those people, in history.

In summary, then, if the religion of which our American culture is the form is the Jewish-Christian, what the historian discovers to be the presuppositions on which its ideology rests ought to be the "metaphysical intuitions" that are apprehended by faith in our churches; articulated in their creeds and confessions; lifted up in worship; and remembered in the sacrament. And in this case we would expect the speculative historian's intellectual quest to lead him to greater and greater appreciation of what the churches have been all about. To my mind this expectation is somewhat borne out by what has happened to, in, and among notable so-called "secular" students of American intellectual, cultural, and social history during the past thirty years. Their work intimates that they have begun to see and to acknowledge the soil in which the presuppositions of this society are rooted. Meanwhile some scholars within the churches seem to be engaged in torpedoing the presuppositions upon which such rapprochement might begin. As the intellectual quest of those historians disdainfully labeled "secular" brings them closer and closer to the Church, some men within the Church seem to be advocating that the Church beat a "strategic retreat," burning the intellectual bridges between them and the "secularists" behind them.

I would prefer to try to meet the advancing "secularists" halfway and wish I were better equipped to do so. At present I can only say that it seems to me that Christians in their churches assert in faith and in figurative language that human history is a meaningful story with beginning, middle, and end— knowable and known in part by man but known completely and ultimately only to God (that is, human history is contingent). The assertion that human history is a meaningful story makes the intellectual quest worthwhile. The assertion that only God knows the final end of the story means that all human constructions of segments of it are limited and tentative. As Herbert Butterfield put it, all histories, even church histories, are but interim reports on the way things look to the author here and now. Hence, while there is never complete assurance of the happy or successful outcome of the story given to man, neither can there be complete despair of the outcome. Complete pessimism and complete optimism are both heresies. This, in turn, means that men must live by faith in the God of the living—that is, the God of those living in history.

And here is a further comment on the historian's pathway to freedom. For granted the assumption that it is the Jewish-Christian religion that has informed our culture, the end of the historian's intellectual quest to understand who and what we most profoundly are, must lead him to the basic precepts of that religion which as Christians we may and do apprehend in faith and celebrate in worship. In either case we arrive at the fullest self-understanding which is our fullest freedom. On these suppositions the paths of both our intellectual and our religious quests lead us to the same point. To the Christian both paths lead to the God preeminently revealed in Jesus Christ, the author of his faith *and* the Lord of all his history. Whichever path he takes implies that he believes that at its end he shall know himself as he is now known only by his Creator. His assertion in faith is a declaration of the primary presupposition of his intellectual quest—"Now my knowledge is imperfect, but then I shall know as fully as God knows me" (I Cor. 13:12).

¹Originally published in *Church History*, XXXII, 1 (March, 1963), 17–31. Reprinted in *New Theology No. 1*, ed. by Martin E. Marty and Dean G. Peerman (New York: The Macmillan Co., 1964), pp. 75–93.
²Charles A. Beard, "Written History as an Act of Faith," *American Historical Review*, XXXIX (January, 1934), 222.

³Clark Kerr in a letter to the editor, *Saturday Review* (October 20, 1962), p. 73.

⁴H. Richard Niebuhr, *The Kingdom of God in America* (Chicago: Willett, Clark & Co., 1937), pp. 12–13.

⁵Alfred North Whitehead, *Adventures of Ideas* (New York: Free Press, 1967), p. 4.

⁶"Theory and Practice in Historical Study: A Report of the Committee on Historiography" (New York: Social Science Research Council, Bulletin 54, 1946), p. 135.

⁷John H. Randall, Jr., and George Haines, IV, "Controlling Assumptions in the Practice of American Historians," in *Ibid.*, pp. 20–21.

⁸*Ibid.*, p. 21 (for both quotations in this paragraph).

⁹*Ibid.* (for all quotations in this paragraph).

¹⁰William Alva Gifford, *The Story of the Faith: A Survey of Christian History for the Undogmatic* (New York: The Macmillan Company, 1946), p. vii.

III AMERICAN HISTORY AS A TRAGIC DRAMA[1]

> Meanwhile, he and these other souls struggled darkly through a series of Events, the imperfect writhings of their human dream. Out of them they built a fiction called the Past and embodied it in a myth called History. . . . And slowly he discovered that in the imperfect world of his personal dream, he had been making the legend of a hero. This hero was Humanity, and the place in which the hero strove for beauty and the good was the Republic. Both Hero and Republic were immense fictions. They could never have existed without their poet, but neither could he have existed without them. . . . And so he learned that Raintree County being but a dream must be upheld by dreamers. So he learned that human life's a myth, but that only myths can be eternal. So he learned the gigantic labor by which the earth is rescued again and again from chaos and old night.[2]

I should like to suggest the plausibility of a tragic conception of what Henry Bamford Parkes so aptly called "the American experience"[3]—to suggest that perhaps Americans can most profoundly understand their collective and dynamic experience on this continent as a tragic drama and themselves as actors in that kind of play. The form of my presentation is determined by two considerations: first, that I wish merely to suggest the plausibility of this interpretive motif—to make what J. H. Hexter called "a modest proposal,"[4] and second, that effectiveness in so doing demands an appeal to the imagination as much as (perhaps more than) the development of an argument.

I

In order to indicate what I mean by the interpretation of American history as a tragic drama some fairly precise definitions are necessary.

The Nature of Tragedy

A tragedy may be defined as a serious story, in which, typically, the leading character is by some inherent limitation brought to a catastrophe that he recognizes. In Greek tragedy the action as a whole was commonly conceived as a manifestation of fate in which the characters were born to be involved. In modern tragedy the catastrophic end of the action is commonly conceived as a result of the free working out of flaws in the individual's character.

The "tragedy" of America would be conceived primarily in the "modern" sense, although (perhaps because of the strong Calvinistic strand in the religious tradition) near-fatalistic outlooks have always been represented.

35

The Nature of Written History

A history is an *interpretation* of the events of the life of a community of people. An interpretation always implies a framework of meaning. A biographer or historian has to choose what he believes to be the beginning and the end of the story he wishes to tell. This in turn means that he forms an opinion of what would be a (or the) desirable consummation of the series of events with which he is dealing, and hence of what would constitute its frustration.[5] A "story" implies a lineal development with meaningful beginning, middle, and end. Implicit in written history is the belief that human life has some ideal consummation.

The totality of unfolding events of human history are in their entirety sc utterly beyond human comprehension as to be to the unselective mind merely a chaos. This, for the reflective historian, is the primordial chaos, over which the inquisitive mind of man continually hovers, bringing order, creating meaning. Granted, then, that any written history as an interpretive story is a selection and arrangement of *some* events out of the totality of events, it can be said that *a* history results from the imposition of a creative mind on primordial chaos—the vast amorphous, unbroken biological continuity of the human race. This chaos is what Lockridge in his novel *Raintree County* calls "the Swamp,"[6] out of which all life emerged and began what Loren Eiseley calls its "Immense Journey." The historian in writing a history follows a method analogous to the wit's instructions for sculpting an elephant—one takes a big block of granite and chips off everything that does not look like an elephant. It is as simple as that. But there are two stern conditions: he has to begin with an exact idea of what an elephant looks like, and he has to have great technical skill to cut off only what does not look like an elephant.

Man is the teller of tales, the creator of stories about himself, and every history, as a story, is a dramatic production created by an artist. What is called the discipline of history is essentially an agreed upon constellation of rules and standards for judging whether and how well the historian-artist has been true to his medium, and how his technical competence is to be rated. My tragic drama of America would be, then, an artistic creation.

The Nature of Artistic Creation

My conception of what is involved in artistic creation is guided primarily by insights gleaned from Dorothy L. Sayers's book, *The Mind of the Maker*,[7] purportedly an exposition of the doctrine of the Trinity by analogy with human acts of artistic creation. Miss Sayers was one of those amazing English authors whose mind and works ranged through history, philosophy, and theology, but who may be best known for some excellent whodunits. It is not surprising that her analogies are drawn primarily from what goes into literary composition.

Let us begin, then, with the image of a "good" book or play and ask, "What does it convey to me and why?" The chances are that it conveys one striking impression in which feeling is inextricably bound up with the rational definition of a "problem." I am thinking, for example, of Ralph Ellison's *Invisible Man*, or of Nathaniel Hawthorne's *Scarlet Letter*. We say sometimes of such a work that it "got under my skin" and mean, I suppose, that it exerts a strange power over us. If now we shift ourselves out of this appreciative mood into an analytical frame of mind, we may ask, "How did the author manage to do this to me?" The striking thing about one of Hawthorne's works is that when we have finished reading it we realize that every part is subservient to the overall structure—that every chapter, every paragraph, every sentence, practically every word is exactly where it is for a reason, and would be out of place anywhere else. It is for this reason that the effect of the work is cumulative from the beginning to the end—every part contributed to bringing the reader to the single overall impression noted above. This cannot be done by coercion—only by persuasion.

At this point, and especially if one has tried to do some serious writing himself, he is likely to get a second strong impression, namely, that it took a fearful amount of sheer energy, concentration, hard work—blood, sweat, and tears if you please—to produce such a work. If we think that such nicety of structure comes easily to those authors who achieve it, we are simply mistaken. It comes through rigid discipline and long grueling practice during which much is rejected. No doubt most great authors have more pages in their wastebaskets than in print.

Analytically, then, we recognize the strange power the work has over us because of the single impression it gives us; we recognize that in the mind of the author there must have been the intention to do just that, and that it took a tremendous amount of energy and disciplined application to shape the medium (in this case, words) to produce that effect.

Now we are in a position to understand Dorothy Sayers's brief schematization of "the mind of the maker" as artist. Every act of creation, she says, is threefold.

First, "there is the Creative Idea, passionless, timeless, beholding the whole work complete at once, the end in the beginning." In this sense the creative idea (the idea of what the "elephant" looks like) is "eternal."

Second, there is "the Creative Energy [or *Activity*] begotten of that idea, working in time from the beginning to the end, with sweat and passion" to incarnate the creative idea "in the bonds of matter." In other words, the creative activity is directed to sculpting the "elephant," that is, to incarnating the creative idea in the chosen medium (words, stone, wood, human beings, etc.). Every medium has a stubborn integrity of its own and resists being used and shaped. This can be overcome only by hard work and highly developed technical skills. In the Christian myth, the archetype of incarnation is the

Word made Flesh, something accomplished only through poignant and terrible suffering.

Third, there is the "Creative Power"—what we call the meaning of the work in terms of the response to it in the observer. The readers perceive the book "both as a process in time and as an eternal whole, and react to it dynamically." Through this product of the creative activity the creative idea is communicated to the readers and "produces a corresponding response in them." The response defines the power of the incarnation to communicate the creative idea back of it.[8]

"The Power" depends upon how successful the attempt has been to incarnate the creator's idea in material form. This judgment on the result is necessarily a qualitative one. It is the judgment as to how fully the incarnation effectively communicates the idea. This judgment, in turn, is based on consideration of the power the finished work has to convey to others what the creator-as-artist had in mind. Therefore a created work may be judged a flop for one or all of several reasons: that the artist lacked the technical skills to master and manage his chosen medium; or he lacked the energy for the work; or he attempted to incarnate the idea in a medium that made it impossible— one cannot, literally, write sonnets in stone, or, it is said, make silk purses out of sows' ears.[9] On the other hand, it is possible that the beholder lacks the capacity to appreciate what he sees.

This way of looking at our history is difficult because it taxes the imagination to conceive of "the people" as, at one and the same time, the artist in whom the creative idea lives; and the medium in which the idea is to be incarnated through their own activity as artist; and the beholder affected by the power of the work; and the critic—analyst and judge—of the results. Nevertheless I think that some such complex perspective is involved in all historical interpretation of one's own community.

I am told that Shakespeare sometimes played a part in one of his own plays. If so, he must have assumed all these roles in relation to it.

Similarly, Lincoln seems to have been conscious of playing all these roles in what he called "the Union," as witness, for example, his address to the New Jersey Senate on February 21, 1861:

> I recollect thinking then, boy even though I was, that there must have been something more than common that those men struggled for [the creative idea]. I am exceedingly anxious that that thing which they struggled for; that something even more than National Independence; that something that held out a great promise to all the people of the world to all time to come; I am exceedingly anxious that this Union, the Constitution, and the liberties of the people shall be perpetuated in accordance with the original idea for which that struggle was made [the creative energy] and I shall be most happy indeed if I shall be an humble instrument in the hands of the Almighty, and of this, his almost chosen people, for perpetuating the object of that great struggle.[10]

To be sure, in Lincoln's mythology God is the artist, and since He is "the Almighty," His will somehow will prevail. But the God of Lincoln does not reveal His will to man through a special revelation. Therefore man knows God's will only through an interpretation of "the plain physical facts" of the unfolding history. In this sense the God of Lincoln's mythology is inseparable from "the people." Man must judge God's will for anticipated action on the basis of his interpretation of "where we are and whither we are tending." But he can know (and then only as through a glass darkly) the will of God only in retrospect—that is, only after the unfolding events of the history-that-happens has revealed in the vicissitudes of these people the results of the decisions made. This is the concept of the judgment of history ("we cannot escape history") which is the judgment of God—the conceptual backbone of the Second Inaugural Address.

Because to Lincoln man's knowledge of what the will of God is at any particular time is always an interpretation of the infinite mind by the finite, no man can know that the almightyness of God guarantees the successful outcome of what he, as man, conceives to be the desirable and decides to do. From the perspective of finite man, Lincoln's God is artist—is perfect creative idea and is awesome energy. "The will of God prevails"—He can and will create the perfect work. Many Christians have concluded from this that their finite conception of the will of God shall prevail. Not so Lincoln. He might have said that no man has any way of knowing that God-as-artist will not give up the attempt to create the perfect work in the present medium—man.[11] This is to say, I suppose, that for Lincoln, God provided no cosmic guarantee for any humanly conceived scheme of values. All man can do is trust "the Almighty" who "has His own purposes" in history—trust that His judgments are indeed "true and righteous altogether," and commend his finite being to God's infinite justice—the theme so prominent in the Second Inaugural Address. This is to say that mankind must live by faith.

From this perspective, men in all their works which constitute the stuff of history are stuck with being artists—artist co-workers with an artist-God—stuck also with the only medium they have, human beings "working just as they do." What is suggested here is a perspective—an overall way of looking at things—that is applicable to the understanding and conduct of whatever work one is called to do—even administration.

My ideal historian is a creative artist. To him written history is a drama, and all the world is a stage upon which men and women play parts—often in a manner to make the angels weep. My historian may look upon American history as a tragic drama if he has the imagination to see (1) that the American experiment grew out of a creative idea of the potential capacity of mankind to be "free"—to have, for example, government by reflection and choice; (2) that for a time at least these people exhibited such creative activity as to justify wise men in hoping that they might successfully incarnate their creative idea—their dream—in actuality;[12] (3) that when the society and life of these people is looked at today *as a work of art*, it lacks "power"—that is, it does not produce in the beholder any clear impression of purpose and meaning; (4) that one concludes that this failure of "power" is due to some flaw inherent in the nature of the medium itself—in other words, a flaw in the available human material, in "the people."[13]

II

The first brief sketch of the creative idea of America appeared in the Declaration of Independence in 1776. The picture was filled in during the following sixty-five years. In this process, images of man, the good (or ideal) society, the government, and destiny were etched into the American character so deeply that they are still the dominant motivational myths of the nation, constantly invoked to stand in judgment over our present devious shenanigans.

The Declaration is a sketch of "all men . . . created equal"—not in the sense that they are equal in talents and potentialities, but in the sense that they are "endowed by their Creator with certain unalienable rights" whatever talents they may possess. An "unalienable right" is not only one that should not be denied a man, but one that he cannot voluntarily refuse to exercise because it is his by nature. Therefore the obverse side of a "right" is a responsibility. It follows that the Declaration's sketch of the rights to "life, liberty and the pursuit of happiness" implies man's duty to seek, find, and perpetuate them. Governments exist only to "secure these rights." A government is an instrument which exists only "by the consent of the governed" for this purpose. If and when it threatens the rights of man as man, it may be altered or abolished and another put in its place. Another way of saying this is that a government exists to free men to exercise their natural rights. This need not imply that the free man is a good man, and that a society of free men will automatically create and maintain an ideal government. This becomes clear in the Constitution, which added to the sketch by incarnating in the system of checks and balances the idea that, because of what Alexander Hamilton called "the ordinary depravity of human nature,"[14] no man is to be trusted with unexamined, unlimited power.

Another dimension of the creative idea, the image of destiny, was noted by Hamilton in the first Federalist Paper. In defense of the proposed Constitution he said,

> It has been frequently remarked that it seems to have been reserved to the people of this country, by their conduct and example, to decide the important question, whether societies of men are really capable or not of establishing good government from reflection and choice, or whether they are forever destined to depend for their political constitutions on accident and force.

The new nation was thus conceived as a great experiment with all the world as the laboratory in which the nature of man was to be tested. The question was, is the nature of man such that he is capable of self-government?

A generation later when the experiment seemed to be turning out so well that even wise men hoped, the very orthodox Rev. Lyman Beecher put the whole idea succinctly:

> The time has come, when the experiment is to be made, whether the world is to be emancipated and rendered happy, or whether the whole creation shall groan and travail together in pain. . . . If it had been the design of Heaven to establish a powerful nation, in the full enjoyment of civil and religious liberty, where all the energies of man might find full scope and excitement, on purpose to show the world by one great successful experiment, of what man is capable . . . where could such an experiment have been made but in this country, . . . The light of such a hemisphere . . . will shine into the darkness . . . and be comprehended, it will awaken desire, and hope, and effort, and produce revolutions and over-turnings, until the world is free.[15]

Finally the idea received its classical expression by Abraham Lincoln at Gettysburg:

> Our fathers brought forth on this continent a new nation, conceived in liberty, and dedicated to the proposition that all men are created equal. Now we are engaged in a great civil war, testing whether that nation, or any nation so conceived and so dedicated, can long endure.

It is clear that Lincoln thought of it as a great experiment, with the final result by no means assured. He had already said, and I suppose he meant it, that "We," the people of this nation, may "nobly save or meanly lose the last, best hope of earth." So at Gettysburg he could not and did not assert with finality that the dead had not died in vain. All he could ask was that

> we here highly resolve that these dead shall not have died in vain; that this nation, under God, shall have a new birth of freedom; and that government of the people, by the people, for the people, shall not perish from the earth.

Meantime, between the Revolution and the Civil War the definition of the creative idea had been rounded out and given some more specific content with the emergence of a constellation of ideas (or images)—of the free individual; of perfection for the individual and for society; of progress; of equality; of voluntaryism; of paternalism.[16]

I suppose that my interpretation stands or falls, not on the adequacy of my understanding and/or the persuasiveness of my presentation of the creative idea of America, but on the plausibility that there was a creative idea (the substance of things hoped for, the evidence of things not seen) which appeared so soundly based that wise men hoped that it could be incarnated in actuality, and that the result would have "power." The plausibility depends not only on the historical evidence, strictly speaking, but also on the feeling that we today, as wise men and women in our generation, may find the creative idea moving within us—may find ourselves capable of being possessed by the dream it evokes of actualizing a better society than man has ever known, and, in spite of all the contrary evidence that history affords, of sometimes almost believing that "we shall overcome." In the present at least we ought to be able to say as we look back upon our history what Nathaniel Hawthorne was moved to say when he looked back upon his experience at Brook Farm:

> Often . . . in these years that are darkening around me, I remember our beautiful scheme of a noble and unselfish life; and how fair, in that first summer, appeared the prospect that it might endure for generations, and be perfected, as the ages rolled away, into the system of a people and a world! . . . More and more I feel that we had struck upon what ought to be a truth [about man and society]. . . . Posterity may dig it up and profit by it.[17]

Hawthorne was groping for a tragic understanding of American history and perhaps he had already touched it.

During the sixty-five years that followed the Declaration, while the full picture of the creative idea was being completed, there was much to support the view that "the people" as artist had the creative energy and the technical skills to incarnate it in actuality.

> The faith of the young Republic seemed to be vindicated. It had separated itself from European control through a successful, albeit conservative, revolution. It had established itself under a Constitution based upon belief in the ability of men to have "good government from reflection and choice". . . . It had not fallen into the trap of aristocratic and possibly reactionary sentiments set by the Federalists being led around it by Thomas Jefferson and his Republican party. . . . It had weathered a second war with England and gained a settlement which a French observer referred to as "the peace that passeth understanding." Nine years later it had issued its second declaration of independence from Europe in President Monroe's famous doctrine. European visitors who earlier had been more inclined to scoff and criticize spitefully . . . now came to admire and even to envy and applaud the great experiment. Alexis de Tocqueville saw in it the shape of things to come in Western culture.[18]

Nature itself seemed to encourage and support the energy resident in these people. The physical setting was bountiful and, relative to population, seemed inexhaustible. In that primarily agrarian economy it provided a rather sure basis of support for individuals and communities, and hence encouraged a high degree of independence and opportunity to experiment almost unchecked by physical limitations. And insofar as America was a frontier of Western civilization, it also gave these people the opportunity to work at incarnating any creative idea they might have with a minimum of outside interference or of restrictions imposed by inherited tradition, custom, and law.

We should not underestimate their achievement. From small beginnings they built a great and powerful nation out of the discarded peoples from every nation on earth. They built it on a vision of a better life than men had ever known. And as the idea began to take shape in actuality, it exerted great power over the Americans themselves, apparently reaching a peak in the 1840s and 1850s. Ralph Waldo Emerson, one of the seers of the time, exulted:

There is a moment in the history of every nation, when, proceeding out of this brute youth, the perceptive powers reach their ripeness and have not yet become microscopic; so that man, at that instant, extends across the entire scale, and with his feet still planted on the immense forces of night, converses by his eyes and brain with solar and stellar creation. That is the moment of adult health, the culmination of power.[19]

This culmination of power was seen as rising from the free but common people. The "august dignity I treat of," wrote Herman Melville in *Moby Dick*,

is not the dignity of kings and robes, but that abounding dignity which has no robed investiture. Thou shalt see it shining in the arm that wields a pick or drives a spike; that democratic dignity which, on all hands, radiates without end from God; Himself!

And so Melville prayed, in defiance of all aristocratic traditions,

If, then, to meanest mariners, and renegades and castaways, I shall hereafter ascribe high qualities, though dark; . . . if I shall touch that workman's arm with some ethereal light; . . . then against all mortal critics bear me out in it, thou just Spirit of Equality, which hast spread one royal mantle of humanity over all my kind! Bear me out in it, thou great democratic God! . . . Thou who didst pick up Andrew Jackson from the pebbles; who didst hurl him upon a warhorse; who didst thunder him higher than a throne! Thou who, in all Thy mighty, earthly marchings, ever cullest Thy selectest champions from the kingly commons; bear me out in it, O God![20]

The release of creative energy during this time is well established. Van Wycks Brooks rightly called his study of the period, *The Flowering of New England*, and Lewis Mumford wrote of it as *The Golden Day*. But perhaps it has been treated most extensively and with greatest insight by F. O. Matthiessen in his *American Renaissance*.[21] "The starting point for this book," said the author, "was my realization of how great a number of our past masterpieces were produced in one extraordinarily concentrated moment of expression." This, he argued, is borne out by the fact that "the half-decade of 1850-55 saw the appearance of *Representative Men* (1850), *The Scarlet Letter* (1850), *The House of the Seven Gables* (1851), *Moby Dick* (1851), *Pierre* (1852), *Walden* (1854), and *Leaves of Grass* (1855). You might search all the rest of American literature without being able to collect a group of books equal to these in imaginative vitality."[22]

How did Matthiessen account for this "extraordinarily concentrated moment of expression"? He wrote, "The one common denominator of my five writers, uniting even Hawthorne and Whitman, was their devotion to the possibilities of democracy." [23] This conclusion is borne out by Arthur Bestor, who has written extensively and with great insight on the period.[24]

The "complex of ideas" which lay back of the numerous communitarian experiments of the time, Bestor concluded, emphasizes the "moral imperative" provided by the sentiment that "men and women were duty bound to seize, while it still existed, the chance of building their highest ideals into the very structure of the future world."[25] This is what I have called their drive to incarnate their creative idea in actuality, in history.

I think one could make an analogous case for the same period as a peak in religious vitality in America by examining the work of such leaders as Lyman Beecher, Leonard Woods, Charles G. Finney, Alexander Campbell, Peter Cartwright, Horace Bushnell, William Ellery Channing, Andrews Norton, Theodore Parker, Orestes Brownson, John Hughes, Francis Wayland, Charles Hodge, John Humphrey Noyes, and even Lorenzo Dow, the crazy "Cosmopolite." To paraphrase Henry Adams, the contrast in intellectual and religious vitality and "power" between these men of the first half of the nineteenth century and the present crop of ministers and denominational leaders in America today is alone enough to disabuse us of any lingering illusions we may have about inevitable progress in this area.

As further evidence of the power of the creative idea to release the energies of these people during the first half of the nineteenth century, I would call attention to the many humanitarian and reform crusades and to the many communitarian experiments launched between 1805 and 1855. These were admirably treated in summary fashion by Alice Felt Tyler in her book so aptly entitled *Freedom's Ferment*.[26]

I would note, finally, the power of this incarnation of the democratic ideal over the people of other lands—especially over what Lyman Beecher called "earth's debased millions."[27] This hardly needs amplification. Much has been written on the "image" of America as the land of freedom (i.e., of "free individuals"), as a moving force among the people of the other nations of the world. So powerful, indeed, was the incarnation, that it brought the millions of immigrants to the United States.

III

The tragic outcome is seen in the facts that the consummation at the present time seems to lack such power to release the creative energies of the people of this nation and of the world as it possessed before the Civil War; that there was only a relatively unimportant lack of materials, resources, ability, and technical skills to account for the failure; and that it is recognized that the failure is due to a flaw inherent in these "almost chosen people" themselves.

To hold this view I accept, on what I think to be sufficient evidence, that there was a creative idea of America that, it was plausible to suppose, might be incarnated in a society because it was based on a realistic view of the nature of man.[28] Insofar as the creative idea is expressed in the one word, "democracy," what I have in mind here was beautifully expressed by Reinhold Niebuhr: "Man's capacity for justice makes democracy possible; but man's inclination to injustice makes democracy necessary."[29]

To be sure, some have, mistakenly I think, questioned the realism and hence the plausibility of the creative idea itself. Among them, for example, D. H. Lawrence, in his *Studies in Classic American Literature*, implied that much of America's dream was never realistic, but at most only "a wish-fulfillment vision, a kind of yearning myth."[30] But, it seems to me, in a sense more profound than the supersophisticated Lawrence was capable of apprehending, all human history might be seen as man's striving toward a "wish-fulfillment vision," and all the Christian religion as a "yearning myth." I would agree with James Branch Cabell who argued in *Beyond Life* that it is only because some men have insisted that man is but little lower than the angels that a few men have lived on a level distinctly above that of the apes.[31] The crucial question is not simply, "Were these people marked by 'a wish-fulfillment vision'?" but, "Was it plausible in their time and place to hope that their vision could be 'tangibilicated,' granted the nature of man?" I think it was, and the tragedy that we recognize is that it failed because of something inherent in the character of the people. James Bryce, in his *The American Commonwealth*, stated it very clearly in the 1890s:

> The government and institutions, as well as the industrial civilization of America, are far removed from the ideal commonwealth which European philosophers imagined, and Americans expected to create.[32]

And this, as Alexander Hamilton predicted, may well "deserve to be considered as the general misfortune of mankind."

I have hinged the definition of tragedy upon the recognition by the tragic hero and the audience (in this case both is "the people") of the nature of and reasons for the catastrophic consummation. Such awareness begins to appear in American history before the Civil War, was greatly accentuated by that event, and flowered in the spread of cynicism following World War I by such characters as F. Scott Fitzgerald's Amory Blaine who, after graduation from Princeton, grew up "to find all Gods dead, all wars fought, all faiths in man shaken . . ."[33]

While many of his contemporaries were exulting in the tremendous growth of their country, its power and prestige in the world, its increasing national prosperity, Henry David Thoreau reminded them that all of this might be merely improved means to an unimproved end. And Walt Whitman, as he looked about him after the Civil War, gloomily contemplated the contrast between the bulging pecuniary and national growth and the concurrent shrinking of the soul:

> The great cities reek with respectable as much as non-respectable robbery and scoundrelism. In fashionable life, flippancy, tepid amours, weak infidelism, small aims, or no aims at all, only to kill time. In business . . . the sole object is, by any means, pecuniary gain . . . The best class we show, is but a mob of fashionably dress'd speculators and vulgarians . . . our New World democracy, however great a success in uplifting the masses out of their sloughs, in materialistic development, products, and in a certain highly-deceptive superficial popular intellectuality, is, so far, an almost complete failure in its social aspects, and in really grand religious, moral, literary, and esthetic results. . . . It is as if we were somehow being endow'd with a vast and more and more thoroughly-appointed body, and then left with little or no soul.[34]

As examples of the widespread awareness of the contrast between the ideal and the actuality pointed out by Thoreau, Whitman, and Bryce, I would note, for example, first the outcome of the many communitarian experiments launched between 1825 and 1860; and second, the aftermath of the Civil War. Both remind us that as articulate people in the society became aware of this contrast they most commonly attributed the failure to a flaw in the character of "the people"—in man himself.

IV

It is estimated that between 1825 and 1860 ninety-six communitarian experiments were launched, fifty-four of them in the decade 1840–49.[35] Actually only an insignificant part of the total population was involved. John Humphrey Noyes, founder and leader of the Oneida Community, estimated that probably they numbered only between 9,000 and 18,000 actual members.[36] But he argued, as does Arthur Bestor, that they were more significant than a mere quantitative glance at the numbers participating might indicate. They were a center of attention. "As Emerson wrote to Carlyle in the Autumn of 1840: 'We are all a little wild here with numberless projects of social reform. Not a reading man but has a draft of a new community in his waistcoat pocket.'"[37] They were banks in which a great deal of the hope and the striving of the period for the "perfect" society were invested, and when they failed, as they all did, many Americans went bankrupt in aspiration and became cynical.

It is important to understand how they were conceived. The inclusive context and the archetypal image of each was, of course, the creative idea of the Republic itself, moving toward the "perfect" society in which individuals could be "free." They were, as Arthur Bestor so aptly called them, "Patent-Office Models of the Good [i.e., the "perfect"] Society," and as Tyler argued, each was launched as a "model for a new and better social order."[38] Therefore the communitarian movement as a whole can well be seen as a microcosmic analogue of the new nation. Each was premised on the supposition so clearly stated by Albert Brisbane in 1843:

> The whole question of effecting a Social Reform may be reduced to the establishment of one Association, which will serve as a model for, and induce the rapid establishment of others. . . . Now if we can, with a knowledge of true architectural principles, build one house rightly, conveniently and elegantly, we can, by taking it for a model and building others like it, make a perfect and beautiful city; in the same manner, if we can, with a knowledge of true social principles, organize one township rightly, we can, by organizing others like it, and by spreading and rendering them universal, establish a true Social and Political Order.[39]

The founders hoped, as each venture was launched, that their community would prove to be the working "patent-office model" of the perfect society.

But each had to be undertaken as an experiment to find out if a society so conceived and operated would really work, and if not, why not. So pervasive was the mood of experimentation that founders of a community were inclined to encourage others to do likewise, as Adin Ballou of the Hopedale Community urged

> each class of dissenting socialists [to] stand aloof from our Republic and experiment to their heart's content on their own wiser systems. . . . It is desirable that they should do so in order that it may be demonstrated as soon as possible which the true social system is.[40]

This was not just an abstract discussion of the nature of the good, or the "perfect" society, but actual experimentation to find out whether or not this or that hypothesis regarding its nature would work in practice. The deep and far-reaching effect of the failure of these ventures on the American character can be realized only if we understand this pragmatic aspect of their conduct. Men are not likely to be deeply affected by inability to maintain their point in an abstract discussion. But when they risk their point in a public demonstration and lose they are likely to be deeply affected.

Because the communities were intended to be models of a perfect society for "free" individuals, they had to be based on the principle of voluntary consent. In such a society radical competition between selfish individuals is wrong in principle. So when these experimenters dreamed of "a society which should be co-operative and not competitive, communal and not individualistic,"[41] the dream was based on a view of the nature of man. This is what was at stake.

What were the results of these experiments? Outwardly it was failure. They all failed sooner or later, most of them sooner: "All died young, and most of them before they were two years old."[42] They failed in practice—they failed to survive.

But insofar as they were experimental attempts to find out what man really is, and hence what must be taken into account by any kind of organization of society, they were not failures. In fact they were awesomely successful. The communitarian ventures demonstrated some of the inescapable aspects of human nature with which any organization must come to terms.

They demonstrated, for example, that competition could not be escaped. As Hawthorne noted the competition of Brook Farm with outside schools and market gardeners, he concluded "that with relation to 'society at large, we stood in a position of new hostility, rather than new brotherhood.'"[43] It was recognized that such competition meant the wielding of coercive power over other persons—perhaps covert rather than overt, but nevertheless real.

The experiments suggested to some the increasing irrelevance of the dominant revivalistic Protestantism to the work of reforming and perfecting society. John Humphrey Noyes, leader of one of the most successful communities, made the ever-widening gulf between the revivalists and what he called the "socialists" a chief theme of his *History of American Socialisms*.[44]

The revivalists, Noyes argued, "had for their great idea the regeneration of the soul," the socialists "the regeneration of society, which is the soul's environment." The separation of the two movements represented for Noyes the departure of Christianity from the great paradigm of Pentecost where, "when the Spirit of truth pricked three thousand men to the heart and converted them . . . its next effect was to resolve them into one family and introduce Communism of property." Thus, he argued, "the greatest of all Revivals was also the great inauguration of Socialism." He concluded that in the nineteenth century "they have both failed in their attempts to bring heaven on earth, *because* they despised each other, and would not put their two great ideas together."[45]

The frightening significance for the Republic of this failure—this increasing separation of religion from the organization of society—was seen in the fact that the experiments demonstrated that only communities based on religious convictions and commitment were likely to succeed. This was the universal conclusion of observers, whether religious or agnostic. Charles A. Dana, in an editorial of 1869, noted that

> communities based upon peculiar religious views have generally succeeded. The Shakers and the Oneida Community are conspicuous illustrations of this fact; while the failure of the various attempts made by the disciples of Fourier, Owen, and others, who have not had the support of religious fanaticism, proves that without this great force the most brilliant social theories are of little avail.[46]

Robert Dale Owen, looking back upon his father's New Harmony Community, attributed its failure "to the lack of belief in a higher power; there was no unity of action, as there was no unity of belief."[47] The conclusion was that a society could not be based merely upon the selfish interests of the individuals composing it, each individual being interested only in what he got out of it, but demanded commitment of every individual in it to a vision that transcended all. Thus a disappointed Fourierist said he had learned that there must be some greater purpose than merely "to fly from the ills that they had already experienced in civilization."[48]

But it was not just that religion provided a transcendent creative idea which, because shared by all, bound the individuals together. Religion seemed also the only force capable of overcoming the gross defect in human character that stood in the way of "association." The socialists without religion, Noyes noted, "as often as they came together in actual attempts to realize their ideals, found that they were too selfish for close organization."[49] Among the leaders of the communities that had failed Noyes observed an "almost entire unanimity" respecting the causes of the failure—"GENERAL DEPRAVITY, all say, is the villain of the whole story"[50]—"human depravity is the dread

'Dweller of the Threshold,' that lies in wait at every entrance to the mysteries of Socialism."[51] Noyes found that eight of the communities were strikingly successful when judged on the basis of duration and relative prosperity, and noted that "the one feature which distinguishes these Communities from the transitory sort, is their religion; which in ever case is of the earnest kind . . . and controls all external arrangements." Therefore he thought it

> a fair induction from the facts before us that earnest religion does in some way modify human depravity so as to make continuous Association possible, and insure to it great material success. Or if it is doubted whether it does essentially change human nature, it certainly improves in some way the *conditions* of human nature in socialistic experiments.[52]

Recognizing this, Noyes rejected the socialistic view that the harmony between individuals necessary for community living was merely the "result of getting vast assemblages" together, and argued that such necessary

> equilibrium of the passions and harmony . . . comes by religion; and the idea is evidently growing in the public mind that religion is the *only* bond of agreement sufficient for family Association. If any dislike this condition, we say: Seek agreement in some other way, till all doubt on this point shall be removed by abundant experiment.[53]

Noyes argued that this posed for Christianity the "great Olympic of the nineteenth century" and that "if it shall turn out . . . that Christianity alone has the harmonizing power necessary to successful Association, then Christianity will at last get its crown."[54] Meantime it would be on trial in the Republic.

In summary, the failure of the communities was most commonly interpreted as demonstrating a failure of unredeemed human nature rather than of material resources, technical skills, or organizational and administrative ability.

A. J. Macdonald, who collected much of the material upon which Noyes built his *History of American Socialisms*, was, says Noyes, "discouraged" when he died. Macdonald's preface to his proposed work—all that was written before he died—bears out Noyes's view: "I performed the task of collecting the materials," he explained, "because I thought I was doing good. At one time, sanguine in anticipating brilliant results from Communism, I imagined mankind better than they are, and that they would speedily practice those principles which I considered so true." However, he added, "The experience of years" had disabused him, and the most he now hoped for was that his work would help to convince some that "it was for Humanity" that these people had labored "to realize that 'better state.'"[55] That they had "imagined mankind better than they are" was, said Noyes, "the final confession of the leaders in the Associative experiments generally."[56]

In February 1841 William Ellery Channing, then sixty-two years old, commented on the prospectus for Adin Ballou's Hopedale Community: "I should die in greater peace could I see in any quarter the promise of a happier organization of society." He had, he said,

> for a very long time dreamed of an association, in which the members, instead of preying on one another and seeking to put one another down . . . should live together as brothers, seeking one another's elevation and spiritual growth. But the [human] materials for such a community I have not seen.[57]

Ballou, looking back years later, still marveled at Channing's prescience, for, he said, "The very difficulties which he . . . pointed out in his letter, we were obliged to encounter . . . and they finally proved too much for our virtue and wisdom."[58] Summing up, Ballou gave as his

> deliberate and solemn conviction that the predominating cause of the failure of the Hopedale Community was a moral and spiritual, not a financial one—a deficiency among its members of those graces and powers of character which are requisite to the realization of the Christian ideal of human society.[59]

It was because the failure undermined his optimistic view of human nature that Ballou felt the deathlike chill that settled upon and almost froze his heart.

Here we touch the element that raises the story of these experiments above the level of innocence or adolescent frustration—where blame for failure is projected onto outside persons or forces—to a level of the recognition of real tragedy inherent in the human condition.

V

Recognition of the failure of human nature was written large in the outcome of the Civil War, which swept all the energies of the Republic into one great crusade to save "the Union." "No one cared anything for reform after the Civil War. All the ardent crusades had been trampled under in the one great crusade of the generation."[60] By common consent the war marks a turning point in every aspect of American history. Under Lincoln's powerful conceptual and political leadership the victors in the fratricidal struggle thought of themselves as fighting to preserve and perpetuate the complex creative idea of a self-transcending nation "conceived in liberty, and dedicated to the proposition that all men are created equal."

Now there is a general consensus that somehow the whole thing backfired—that the war to save "the Union" really destroyed it. Ross Lockridge's hero-veteran realized that we "lost the early Republic of our agrarian dream. We fought for it in battle—and destroyed the thing we fought for."[61] As "he sat bemused in theatres, assassins leaped from the wings," and "while he marched in parades, a victor among victors, his postwar dreamworld (which was really his pre-war dreamworld) expired in agony and became a legend on a [tomb]stone."[62]

"The people" is the tragic hero of this drama. For despite the clarity and power of Lincoln's articulation of the creative idea, the tremendous energy that was drawn out of the people in its defense, and the activity and technical skill they exhibited in its conduct, the shape of the "work" after the war either lacked power, or showed a demonic dimension by having a power contrary to the dream of the artist-people. Here is the nub of the tragedy. It lies, not in the great technological and material development as such, and not even in the simple fact that the actuality of America appeared more and more ugly and less and less the progressive incarnation of the ideal. Rather it lay in the fading from the mind of the artist-people of the creative idea—the evaporation of their dream. Lacking leaders with the imagination to picture and the intellectual vigor to articulate the creative idea, the artist-people lost sight of what "the elephant" looked like, and this sapped their moral energy to continue to chip away everything that did not look like their "elephant." This may be what Emerson anticipated when he spoke of things being in the saddle and riding mankind. But deep within them lingered the folk's intuitive knowledge, born out of the past experience of the race and the nation, that this time the failure resulted from a dimension of their own nature.

Of course the ideal "Republic" dreamed by the founders never existed in actuality—could never exist completely—as every artist should know. It was a vision, an artist-people's creative idea that imbued them with the Energy to strive—and with considerable success—to incarnate it in actuality. When, following the Civil War, the actuality was seen increasingly to be at odds with the vision, the prevailing tendency in the name of a grimy "realism" was to relinquish belief in all such visions and cease to dream. From the artist's perspective this is the fatal fallacy. For he knows that the value of a creative idea is not to be judged by the ability, technical skills, and energy he can muster to incarnate it. William Faulkner's words were spoken to all the artist-people who have dreamed of a better world:

> By artist I mean of course everyone who has tried to create something which was not here before him, with no other tools and material than the uncommerciable ones of the human spirit; who has tried to carve, no matter how crudely, on the wall of that final oblivion, in the tongue of the human spirit, "Kilroy was here."
> This is primarily, and I think in its essence, all that we ever really tried to do. And I believe we will all agree that we failed, that what we made never quite matched—never will match the shape, the dream of perfection which we inherited—which drove us—will continue to drive us, even after each failure, until anguish frees us and the hand falls still at last.[63]

[1]Originally published in *Journal of Religion*, LII (October, 1972), 336–60.
[2]Ross Lockridge, Jr., *Raintree County* (Boston: Houghton Mifflin Co., 1948), pp. 1020–21.
[3]Henry Bamford Parkes, *The American Experience: An Interpretation of the History and Civilization of the American People* (New York: Vintage Books, 1959).

[4]"We have got so habituated to grandiose claims, that a modest proposal is unlikely to be much heeded; and one achieves the apotheosis implied by the designation 'seminal mind' only by propounding at great length and with excessive elaboration universal solutions demonstrated false in the end only by the wearisome toil of scores of investigators or by the slow anguish of bitter experience." J. H. Hexter, *Reappraisals in History* (Evanston, IL: Northwestern University Press, 1961), p. 207.

[5]"Even when he has rigorously confined himself to one selected aspect, political or cultural" the historian "still depends on some decision as to what constitutes the culmination of that phase of human experience and as to what constitutes its degradation." A. N. Whitehead, *Adventures of Ideas* (New York: Free Press, 1967), p. 4.

[6]Lockridge, p. 932.

[7]Dorothy L. Sayers, *The Mind of the Maker* (New York: Living Age Books, 1956), pp. 47ff.

[8]In Christendom the archetypal image of this response is found in Mark 15:39: "And when the centurion . . . saw that he so cried out, and gave up the ghost, he said, Truly this man was the Son of God."

[9]See, e.g., Sayers, chap. 10, "Scalene Trinities."

[10]Roy P. Basler, ed., *The Collected Works of Abraham Lincoln* (New Brunswick, NJ: Rutgers University Press, 1953), 4:236.

[11]In the light of what is now known about the extinction of species, this makes a great deal of sense.

[12]"Within this period [roughly 1750–1850] one essential quality stimulated all sociological functionings. That quality was hope—not the hope of ignorance. The peculiar character of this central period was that wise men hoped, and that as yet no circumstance had arisen to throw doubt upon the grounds of such hope" (A. N. Whitehead, "The Study of the Past—Its Uses and Its Dangers," in *Essays in Science and Philosophy* [New York: Philosophical Library, 1948], p. 114). Borrowing from Whitehead, I developed this theme in chap. 6 of *The Lively Experiment* (New York: Harper & Row, 1963), pp. 90–102.

[13]"The people" is an abstract concept pointing to the unbroken biological continuity of the human race which is neither good nor evil, neither moral nor immoral, but just *is*. "The people" is the flood upon which all culture floats—the chaos over which and in which the eternal creative spirit moves, separating light from darkness, good from evil—building islands of rationality and order, of truth, beauty, and goodness, on the dark amorphous sea of life. "The people" is everyman and no man—everyone and no one.

One of the most striking presentations of the idea of the flaw inherent in these people is in Adlai E. Stevenson's 1959 lecture in memory of A. Powell Davies, "Our Broken Mainspring." Said Stevenson, "I am not worried about our various pieces—our technology, our science, our machines, our resources. But I am concerned, desperately concerned about our mainspring. That it has run down, we know. But is it broken; is it broken beyond repair? In the last analysis, no question is worth more consideration in America today." Stuart Gerry Brown, *Adlai E. Stevenson, A Short Biography: The Conscience of the Country* (Woodbury, NY: Barron's Woodbury Press, 1965), pp. 205–6.

[14]Clinton Rossiter, ed., *The Federalist Papers* (New York: A Mentor Book, 1961), no. 78, p. 471; and no. 1, p. 33. It is this realistic view of human nature that keeps the Creative Idea of the Republic from being utopian. "Utopianism" means a view of a new and better society, the achievement of which depends upon effecting a radical change in human nature. Lincoln was clear on this point when, in the Cooper Institute address of February 7, 1860, he said that "human action can be modified to some extent, but human nature cannot be changed." It is this dimension that D. H. Lawrence ignored when he commented that "America's dream was never realistic" (see below, n. 30). Dorothy Sayers's comment, apparently borrowed from Reinhold Niebuhr, is pertinent: "[Utopian theory] imagines that perfect innocency, a new childhood, lies at the end of the social process. It thinks itself capable of creating a society in which all tensions are resolved and the final root of human anarchy is eliminated" (*The Mind of the Maker*, p. 219).

[15]Lyman Beecher, "The Memory of Our Fathers" [1827], in *Sermons Delivered on Various Occasions* (Boston: T. R. Marvin, 1828), pp. 313, 301–2, 304.

[16]I have explained these ideas or images at some length in chap. 6 of *The Lively Experiment.*

[17]Nathaniel Hawthorne, *The Blithedale Romance*, in *The Complete Novels and Selected Tales of Nathaniel Hawthorne*, ed. Norman Holmes Pearson (New York: Modern Library, 1937), p. 584.

[18]*The Lively Experiment*, pp. 90–91.

[19]Ralph Waldo Emerson, *Representative Men: Seven Lectures* (Boston: Houghton Mifflin & Co., 1891), p. 48.

[20]Herman Melville, *Moby Dick: Or the Whale* (New York: Modern Library, 1944), pp. 166, 166–67.

[21]F. O. Matthiessen, *American Renaissance: Art and Expression in the Age of Emerson and Whitman* (New York: Oxford University Press, 1941).

[22]*Ibid.*, p. vii. To Matthiessen's list I would add Harriet Beecher Stowe's *Uncle Tom's Cabin* (1852).

[23]Matthiessen, p. ix.

[24]Arthur Bestor, *Backwoods Utopias: The Sectarian and Owenite Phases of Communitarian Socialism in America· 1663–1829* (Philadelphia: University of Pennsylvania Press, 1950).

[25]Arthur Bestor, "Patent-Office Models of the Good Society," *American Historical Review* 58 (April 1953), 505–26.

[26]Alice Felt Tyler, *Freedom's Ferment: Phases of American Social History to 1860* (Minneapolis: University of Minnesota Press, 1944).

[27]We are reminded of the continuing power of this incarnation over people in other countries by such works as R. L. Bruckberger's *Image of America* (New York: Viking Press, 1964). More striking is the account given by Carlo Levi in his "story of a year" spent while banished to a primitive village in a remote province of southern Italy. "But what never failed to strike me most of all—and by now [because he was a doctor] I had been in almost every house—were the eyes of the two inseparable guardian angels that looked at me from the wall over the bed. On one side was the black, scowling face, with its large, inhuman eyes, of the Madonna of Viggiano; on the other a colored print of the sparkling eyes, behind gleaming glasses, and the hearty grin of President [Franklin D.] Roosevelt. I never saw other pictures or images than these: not the King nor the Duce, nor even Garibaldi; no famous Italian of any kind, nor any one of the appropriate saints; only Roosevelt and the Madonna of Viggiano never failed to be present. . . . Sometimes a third image formed, along with these two, a trinity: a dollar bill, the last of those brought back from across the sea, or one that had come in the letter of a husband or relative, was tacked up under the Madonna or the President, or else between them, like the Holy Ghost or an ambassador from heaven to the world of the dead." *Christ Stopped at Eboli: The Story of a Year* (New York: Noonday Press, 1963), p. 122.

[28]Keeping in mind that "great ideas enter into reality with evil associates and with disgusting alliances. But the greatness remains, nerving the race in its slow ascent." Whitehead, *Adventures of Ideas*, p. 18.

[29]Reinhold Niebuhr, *The Children of Light and the Children of Darkness* (New York: Charles Scribner's Sons, 1945), p. xi.

[30]D. H. Lawrence, *Studies in Classic American Literature* (New York: Viking Press, 1968), p. 51. In fairness to Lawrence it should be noted that he saw that "when one considers [these elements] . . . as presentations of a deep subjective desire" they are "real in their way, and almost prophetic." Walter Allen, probably reflecting Lawrence's view, says that "in *The Great Gatsby* Scott Fitzgerald shows us the American Dream in its tragic aspect, in other words, as a dream incapable of realization precisely because it is a dream" (Walter Allen, *The Urgent West: The American Dream and Modern Man* [New York: E. P. Dutton & Co., 1969], pp. 10–11). This would seem to make dreaming itself tragic—a rather shallow perspective. What is involved here is a hypothesis respecting how one is to account for change in human history. And here A. N.

Whitehead seems eminently more convincing. Arguing that "mankind is not wholly dumb, and in this respect it differs from other races of animals," he suggested that it is always a combination of "senseless agencies and formulated aspirations" (Sayers's "Creative Idea"; Cabell's "Romance") that "cooperate in the work of driving mankind from its old anchorage." By definition the ideal is never perfectly incarnated in actuality, but "the greatness remains, nerving the race in its slow ascent" (*Adventures of Ideas*, pp. 15, 26). To Lawrence "wish-fulfillment" myths are "an evasion of actuality" (Lawrence, p. 52). To Whitehead, as "formulated aspirations" they are the motive force in history.

[31]James Branch Cabell anticipated Whitehead's "slow issue of general ideas into practical consequences" (*Adventures of Ideas*, p. 20) in his whimsical account of "romance": "Romance tricks him, but not to his harm. For, be it remembered that man alone of animals plays the ape to his dreams. Romance it is undoubtedly who whispers to every man that life is not a blind and aimless business, not all a hopeless waste and confusion; and that his existence is a pageant (appreciatively observed by divine spectators), and that he is strong and excellent and wise: and to romance he listens, willing and thrice willing to be cheated by the honeyed fiction. The things of which romance assures him are very far from true: yet it is solely by believing himself a creature but little lower than the cherubim that man has by interminable small degrees become, upon the whole, distinctively superior to the chimpanzee . . . for it is about to-morrow and about the day after to-morrow, that romance is talking by means of parables. And all the while man plays the ape to fairer and yet fairer dreams, and practice strengthens him at mimicry." James B. Cabell, *Beyond Life* (New York: Robert M. McBride & Co., 1921), pp. 356–57.

[32]James Bryce, *The American Commonwealth* (New York: Macmillan Co., 1908), 2:870.

[33]*This Side of Paradise* (New York: Charles Scribner's Sons, 1970), p. 282.

[34]Walt Whitman, *Democratic Vistas, and Other Papers* (London: Walter Scott, 1888), pp. 12–13.

[35]Bestor, *Backwoods Utopias*, p. 243.

[36]John Humphrey Noyes, *History of American Socialisms* (New York: Hillary House Publishers, 1961), p. 22.

[37]As in Alice Felt Tyler, *Freedom's Ferment: Phases of American Social History to 1860*, p. 166.

[38]See n. 25 and Tyler's *Freedom's Ferment*, p. 166.

[39]Quoted in Bestor, "Patent-Office Models," p. 506. The idea of the working model of the good society of course goes back to the first planting of English colonies in America. See, e.g., Perry Miller, *Orthodoxy in Massachusetts 1630–1650: A Genetic Study* (Cambridge, MA: Harvard University Press, 1933); and his article, "Errand into the Wilderness," in the collection of essays published under that title by the Belknap Press of the Harvard University Press in 1956. The essay was first published in the *William and Mary Quarterly* in January 1953.

[40]Quoted in Tyler, p. 169.

[41]V. F. Calverton, *Where Angels Dared to Tread* (Indianapolis: Bobbs-Merrill Co., 1941), p. 17. The paragraphs are worth quoting: "These groups dreamed of an America in which men might be able to carve out the contours of a new society—a society which should be co-operative and not competitive, communal and not individualistic. They were not all of America, but they were an important part of it and their philosophy represents as much of the American dream as the competitive philosophy of the rest of the country. America cannot be understood without understanding their role in its making, for it very well may be that ultimately, before this century is ended, it will be their philosophy, and not the individualistic one, which shall triumph."

[42]Noyes, p. 20.

[43]Mattheissen, n. 21 above. Similarly the cooperative Shaker farmers were in competition with those about them, as were the people of Oneida Community in competition with other makers of traps and silverware.

[44]Noyes, chaps. 3, 47, 48.

[45]*Ibid.*, pp. 26–27. Adin Ballou, leading spirit of the Hopedale Community, agreed that "the notion . . . of a social regeneration corresponding to a regeneration of personal character and life, is quite foreign to the thought, the aspiration, and the specific aim of the average church member of this age," and is "quite above and beyond the apprehension of the common religious teacher of divine truth, save as a beautiful theory." W. S. Heywood, ed., *History of the Hopedale Community, from Its Inception to Its Virtual Submergence in the Hopedale Parish* (Lowell, MA: Thompson & Hiss, 1897), pp. 355–56.

[46]Quoted in Noyes, pp. 138–39.

[47]Marguerite Young, *Angel in the Forest* (New York: Charles Scribner's Sons, 1945), p. 266. As another observer put it, "The internal affinities of Robert Owen's Commune . . . were too weak to resist the attractions of the outer world" (*Ibid.*, p. 264).

[48]Quoted in Noyes, p. 649.

[49]*Ibid.*, p. 27.

[50]*Ibid.*, p. 646.

[51]*Ibid.*, p. 653.

[52]*Ibid.*, p. 655.

[53]*Ibid.*, p. 672.

[54]*Ibid.*, p. 672. Charles Nordhoff agreed with Noyes in general, but would give more emphasis to the negative factor: "I believe that success depends—together with a spiritual religion leavening the mass—upon another sentiment—upon a feeling of the unbearableness of the circumstances in which they [the members] find themselves. The general feeling of modern society is blindly right at bottom: communism is a mutiny against society." *The Communistic Societies of the United States from Personal Visit and Observation. . . .* (New York: Hillary House Publishers, 1961; originally published 1875), p. 408.

[55]Noyes, pp. 8–9.

[56]*Ibid.*, pp. 27–28.

[57]Adin Ballou, *History of the Hopedale Community*, pp. 42, 44, 354–55. [William Ellery Channing] *Memoir of William Ellery Channing with Extracts from His Correspondence and Manuscripts* (Boston: Crosby, Nichols, & Co., 1848), 3:122, 119.

[58]Heywood, p. 45.

[59]*Ibid.*, p. 361.

[60]Lockridge, *Raintree County*, p. 1020.

[61]*Ibid.*, p. 1030.

[62]*Ibid.*, p. 1045.

[63]National Book Award Address, New York, January 25, 1955, in *Saturday Review*, July 28, 1962, p. 25. The idea was stated by George Wald with different imagery and language: "We once represented a kind of beacon light to the world, and all the world looked to us for things that Americans were proud of and I hope will be proud of again—our sense of human liberty, justice, generosity. I think we no longer quite represent these things as we did, but rather great wealth, great power, great greed . . . a great many fundamental changes need to be made—so fundamental as to constitute a continuance of the American Revolution. No revolution is permanent and we need to renew ours." Quoted on the cover of *The Churchman* (August-September 1971), from *Look*, July 13, 1971.

IV ON THE MEANING OF HISTORY[1]

The question, "What is the meaning of history?" makes me feel as Augustine must have felt when to the man who asked, "What was God doing before he made heaven and earth?" he was tempted to reply: "He was preparing hell for those who pry too deep." But, perhaps because he was of saintly stature, Augustine decided it would be better to reply, "I do not know what I do not know" than to "cause one who asked a deep question to be ridiculed."

Augustine here suggests the way I answer the question, "What is the meaning of history?"—namely, I do not know and I know that I do not know. But I would add that saying *I* do not know the meaning of history is not the same as saying history has no meaning. For surely God knows the meaning of history. Man is not God and therefore cannot know the meaning as God does. But he can live by faith in God without knowing all that is in the mind of God regarding his own and mankind's ultimate destiny.

The Christian believes that the Author of the drama in which he is playing a part (without having seen what follows in the script) appeared in one climactic act and said, Fear not, for I am with you. The Christian calls this the incarnation—the metaphysical basis for supposing that an event in the historical drama may contain a clue to what the Author has in mind for the final act and hence a suggestion of how the human individual is to play the part assigned him in his brief scene.

But some today seem to suppose that the Author speaks to them in a very special way in order to let them know what the play looks like to Him from a vantage point outside the theater. They then imagine that they see the play not from the standpoint of their fellow finite actors but from the standpoint of the Author himself, with whom they tacitly identify themselves and become cosmic name droppers.

Often what appears today as the question, "What is the meaning of history?" should be resolved into the general question, "What is the nature of and what are the limits of man's knowledge?" and into the specific question, "Does God give to the Christian a knowledge of history akin to His own?" I cannot here enter into discussion of these questions; it is sufficient to assert that such discussion does not have to begin with the assumption that the answer to the specific question is Yes. To begin thus would seem to destroy the possibility of dialogue between Christians so self-conceived and all others and to make of "theology" not the explanation and defense of the Christian way of

57

life but the caressing of the woolly heads of sheep already in the theologian's fold.

One author (who, please note, seems convinced that he knows with God what the "divine economy" is) summarizes "the Christian view" thus: "In the process of this divine economy everything is from God and to God through Jesus Christ as the mediator." Hence "the pattern of history" is "one great detour to reach in the end the beginning through ever repeated acts of rebellion and self-surrender." From this point of view "the profane events before and after Christ are not a solid chain of meaningful successions but spurious happenings whose significance or insignificance is to be judged in the perspective of their possible signification of judgment and salvation."[2] The implication is that all of man's decisions in the time-contained area of "profane events" are unimportant, meaningless, perhaps evil as such—so far as the "divine economy" is concerned—and that being a Christian enables one to see human history from the perspective of the infinite God.

Erich Auerbach in his *MIMESIS* contrasts this view—which he calls "Christian"—with that of "modern· realism," from which it "differs completely." The former may, he asserts, "altogether dispense with any knowledge" of the "direct earthly connection" between occurrences.[3]

I am not concerned to defend "modern realism" (in which modern history is rooted) against this "Christian" view—although it seems obvious that one cannot have both unless consistency be jettisoned. But it is arrogant to suppose that this is the only Christian view and hence that Christianity advances it as the only option. Indeed, it can be argued that the "modern realism" of practicing historians is rooted in a Christian view of creation and of "ordinary providence."

But the cosmic name droppers circumvent doctrines which provide a premise for supposing some connection between knowledge of events in time and knowledge of God. For them God dwells in an eternal realm, man dwells in time and, as has been argued, salvation comes by "the destruction of time through the contemplation of the eternal." "Potential evil is *in* time: potential good isn't"—"actual good is outside time"—writes Aldous Huxley.[4] And W. H. Auden, says Franklin Baumer, "largely it would seem as a result of the impact of catastrophic world events upon him and the influence of two religious thinkers, Søren Kierkegaard and Reinhold Niebuhr, . . . concluded that 'in Time we sin'"; thereafter with T. S. Eliot he "focused on the way out" of the earthly "wasteland" and "into timelessness."[5] Sometimes our humorists exhibit a great deal of theological insight, and here I am reminded of the cartoon with the caption, "Stop the world, I want to get off!" The attitude suggests a yielding to the temptation the serpent dangled before the original couple—to be like God *now*.

Carl Michalson, swinging freely on (or in) *The Hinge of History*, expounds a conception of "inner history" and "outer history" that appears not only to undermine "modern realism" and the discipline of history but also to make highly dubious his protestation that his view is not "a threat to the embodiment affirmed in Christian realities." For he holds that "inner history simply brackets out the question of the empirical outer-historical existence of christological and ecclesiological realities."[6]

From Michalson's point of view "the embodied church. . . seen by inner history is not the same church [in essence?] as the embodied church seen by outer history." And "inner history asserts that the embodiment of Christ and the church simply cannot be grasped by the methods of outer history." This anthropomorphization of the concept muddies the issue; presumably Michalson is talking about people—insiders who are Christians, outsiders who are not—and asserting that outsiders cannot understand what the insiders do simply because the insiders *say* they cannot. This assertion, aside from being the absolute defense against all criticism and hence a fertile seedbed for obscurantism, illustrates the premise that becoming a Christian adds a god-like epistemological dimension to one's life.

How does one become an "insider"? Mr. Michalson suggests that one should accept "guidance from the inexact," for "the ambiguous and unknowable character of that sphere of reality which remains after science [including all the modern sciences of man?] has made its investigations is a kind of invitation to faith." In that smoggy intellectual atmosphere of the inexact, the ambiguous and the unknowable one may cross "the boundary or frontier or limit in the relation between God and man." But "one knows he is up against it not by objective marks at the frontier but by the tremor in his being. Like the boundary which marks off the stratosphere, he knows he is about to transgress it [and become God?] by the sense of suffocation in his spirit."[7] The ideal religious experience is suggested by "a student who every time he stood next to his girl friend in the dining hall (sensing "her tremendous mystery") felt nauseated," and the ultimate example seems to be "Saint John of the Cross [who] every time [he] had a mystical vision of God . . . vomited."[8]

I am reminded of a remark once made by my wife's aged grandmother. When told that Miss So-and-So was so overpowered by the Spirit at a revival meeting the night before that she got all choked up, Grandma snorted, albeit with compassion, "The poor child has asthma!" Grandma here suggested a serious question which theologians have discussed at length under variations of the rubric "the distinguishing marks of a work of the Spirit of God."Not so Mr. Michalson's "insiders." Perhaps they would "know" it was the Spirit by a sympathetic "sense of suffocation" in their spirits. But they would provide no premises for a discussion of the matter even with fellow Christians. As pictured by Michalson, they deny appeal to an objective reference and dispose of troublesome intellectual problems in a quite different way. Take, for example, the question of miracles.

To the insider, Michalson explains, a miracle "is not a fact of nature" (if it were "it would contribute to the body of knowledge that sooner or later gets around to everyone"!) but "a crack in nature, an absence which man is free to interpret as God's presence" and to exercise toward it "his personal freedom to choose its meaning for himself." Michalson implies that with "the help of science" one might "be certain when some crack in nature called a miracle is a valid support in reality and not a mere projection of the human desire." But he passes over the distinction—and the help of knowledge—in favor of equating the insider's desire with reality. "The question to ask of a miracle . . . is not 'Can you be certain of it?' but 'Can you *be* without it?'"⁹ This umpire insists that the balls pitched are what he calls them! Here again one notes the confusion of the Christian with God.

When he turns to the relationship between Christianity and the discipline of history, Michalson asserts that "the historical question at the heart of the Christian movement is not whether Jesus of Nazareth ever lived but whether there can be a history without him."¹⁰ Perhaps one ought to interpret this sentence as an "invitation to faith" and let it go at that—for it is amazingly ambiguous and inexact. In what sense is this a "historical" question at all? Is the phrase "whether Jesus of Nazareth ever lived" equivalent to "whether the Word was made flesh?" Perhaps it is unimportant for the Christian "whether Jesus of Nazareth ever lived." But is not his belief very important for him that somewhere, sometime, someone lived in history who was very man and very God? But for Mr. Michalson "there is no knowledge of the word of God" to be found in "dated facts."¹¹

It comes as no surprise, therefore, that as theologian he declares war on the historian's history by saying: "It becomes a major theological burden . . . continually to bracket out the 'quest of the historical Jesus' which is conducted in the old style, the world-historical style, in order to elevate to prominence the quest for Jesus as the presence of God and thus the source of the new age."¹² His apparent afterthought that "this is not to deny the relevance of what is being done by conscientious Christian scholars devoted to documentary and archaeological research" sounds lame indeed.¹³ Surely on his premises what such scholars are doing has no relevance for man's quest for "the presence of God." Their attempt to be exact and unambiguous would in itself be sufficient to rule them out. In Löwith's phrase, they are dealing only with "spurious happenings," and Michalson's insider is told to "bracket out" any troublesome empirical reality such scholars may call to his attention—or to stuff it into a convenient crack and exercise "his personal freedom to choose its meaning for himself." Was Nietzsche's madman right? Is the Lord who said "come let us reason together" really dead? Are we left to grope in a vast inexact-ambiguous-unknowable, hoping for a tremor in our being, a sense of suffocation in our spirit, supposing that anything we think we cannot be without *is*?

I have tried to picture what a currently popular, self-styled "Christian" view of history looks like to one practicing historian. I am diffident about trying to present an alternative because, with Sir Thomas Browne, I feel "I have no Genius to disputes in Religion, and have often thought it wisdom to decline them, especially upon a disadvantage, or when the cause of Truth might suffer in the weakness of my patronage."[14] Perhaps that is why I choose to begin by taking refuge behind the massive bulk of G. K. Chesterton, and with him asserting the belief that

> Christianity came into the world firstly in order to assert with violence that a man had not only to look inwards, but to look outwards, to behold with astonishment and enthusiasm a divine company and a divine captain. The only fun of being a Christian was that a man was not left alone with the Inner Light [like Michalson's "insiders"] but definitely recognized an outer light, fair as the sun, clear as the moon, terrible as an army with banners.[15]

I would also agree with Chesterton that it is Christian to suppose that "the ultimate and absolute evil [is] the refusal to take the oath of loyalty to life"[16] (I take "life" and "existence" as being the equivalent of what Michalson calls the "empirical outer-historical . . . realities"). In other words, the sin of sins is the refusal to accept one's finite state and be truly man. I hold this view because, to me, the incarnation means that somehow God is so related to the events of the history-that-happens that the study of their direct earthly connection contains the promise of knowledge of Him.

This is, to be sure, but one side of the matter. The other side has to do with the conviction that the God incarnate in history is the transcendent Creator and that "He who made the world still governs it." Therefore the Christian's faith is in God, not in a knowledge of the events and their connections as such. But the Christian loves the world of these realities because God loved it enough to enter it as a man. Thus, as Chesterton says, Christianity provided "a way of loving the world without trusting it," showed the convert how to "love the world without being worldly."[17]

It is this insight that appears to be lacking in the men I cited above. They seem paralyzed with the thought of the risk involved in supposing God is moving in the events of history. They seem so fearful of risking the ark of God in a battle with the Philistines that they make defeat a premise of their position and in anticipation cry out, "Ichabod, thy glory will depart!" But it might legitimately be concluded from the story in I Samuel 4 and 5 that the God of Israel was able to take care of himself. And a Christian may ask, "Is the Father of our Lord Jesus Christ any less able, O men of little faith?"

Chesterton puts the point beautifully: "Alone of all creeds, Christianity has added courage to the virtues of the Creator."[18] The incarnation suggests that God Himself had the courage to become flesh, to feel as a man feels and to be tempted in all things as a man is tempted. "In that terrific tale of the Passion there is a distinct emotional suggestion that the author of all things (in some unthinkable way) went not only through agony, but through doubt."[19] He was very man as well as very God. And so the lonely cry of the Galilean peasant forsaken of men contained "the cry which confessed that God was forsaken of God."[20]

In the paradox of the incarnation the Christian may find assurance that a clue to the meaning of history resides in the events of the history-that-happens. For him there should be no "profane events," no "spurious happenings." He might say that what God has cleansed at such fearful cost is not for him to call common or unclean. As the incarnation suggests that a man cannot do good or evil "unto one of the least of these" without doing it unto God, so it also suggests that he cannot touch one of the least of these events without touching God.

Those who so believe find the courage to live in time as God did—and does. Their quest for salvation will not be a whining attempt to escape from time into timelessness. It is said that the man-God in agony prayed in the garden, "If it be possible, let this cup pass from me: nevertheless not as I will, but as thou wilt"—and the cup did not pass. Even *His* desire was checked by an objective reality. For the same reason, salvation for the courageous cannot depend on the "bracketing out" of any of earth's empirical outer-historical realities as, some say, it is the prerogative of "insiders" to do. For the Creator is an outsider as well as an insider and he who brackets out realities brackets out God.

What then is the meaning of history? The Christian knows that he does not know. But he believes that God knows and his faith is in God, not in his own knowledge, tremors or sense of suffocation. He believes that on the path through history one encounters Jesus Christ—very man and very God—the Author of his faith and the Lord of all his history. And at the end of his intellectual quest—the study of the empirical realities—he trusts that we shall know ourselves as now he believes in faith that we are known by Him. He loves God with all his rational mind and with all his healthy, unsuffocated spirit. He affirms with Paul, "Now my knowledge is imperfect, but then I shall know as fully as God knows me" (I Cor. 13:12). But this is not a claim to knowledge of the future, but a belief affirmed in faith, and as such always to be made in the context of the prayer, "Lord, I believe; help thou mine unbelief," or, as in the New World translation, "I have faith! Help me out where I need faith!" (Mark 9:24).

[1]Originally published in *The Christian Century*, LXXVII (November 15, 1961), 1361–64.
[2]Karl Löwith, *Meaning in History* (Chicago: University of Chicago Press, 1949), p. 181.
[3]*MIMESIS: The Representation of Reality in Western Literature*, trans. by Willard R. Trask (Garden City, NY: Doubleday Co., 1957), p. 490.
[4]*Religion and the Rise of Scepticism* (New York: Harcourt, Brace, 1960), pp. 264–66.
[5]*Ibid.*, p. 265.
[6]*The Hinge of History: An Existential Approach to the Christian Faith* (New York: Charles Scribner's Sons, 1959), p. 33.

[7]*Ibid.*, pp. 73, 157.

[8]*Ibid.*, pp. 154–55.

[9]*Ibid.*, pp. 75–77.

[10]*Ibid.*, p. 180.

[11]*Ibid.*, p. 183.

[12]*Ibid.*, p. 185.

[13]*Ibid.*, pp. 180–81.

[14]Sir Thomas Browne, *Religio Medici* (first published 1642, 1643); in Norman Endicott, ed., *The Prose of Sir Thomas Browne* (New York: W. W. Norton & Co., 1972), p. 11.

[15]*Orthodoxy* (New York: Dodd, Mead & Co., 1908), p. 76.

[16]*Ibid.*, p. 72.

[17]*Ibid.*, p. 79.

[18]*Ibid.*, pp. 137–38.

[19]*Ibid.*, p. 138.

[20]*Ibid.*, p. 138.

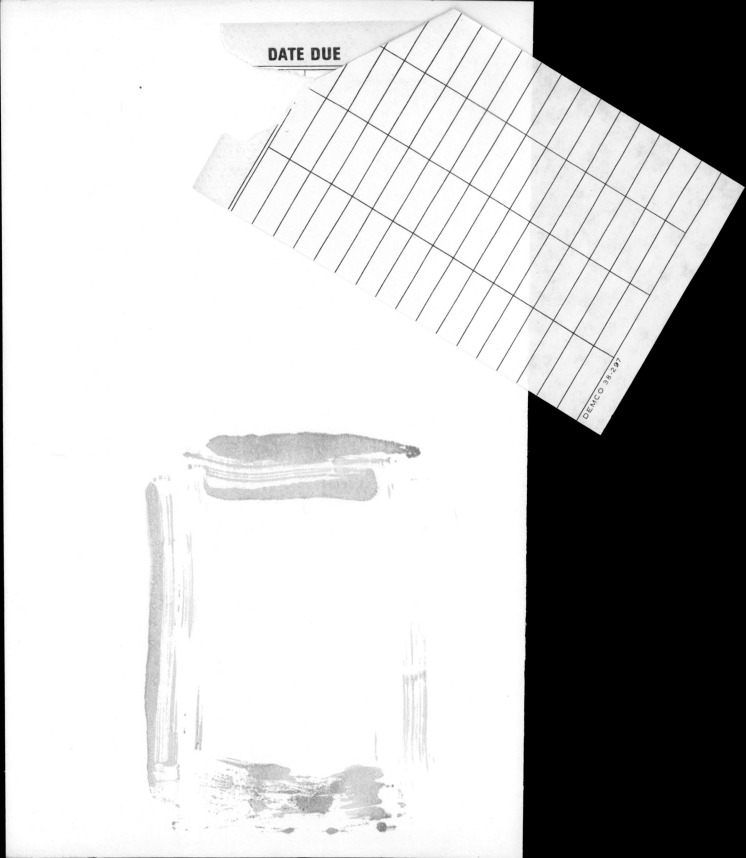